Welcome to our wonderful coloring book designed for children!

Within these fun-filled pages, you will discover a world of artistic possibilities that will let your imagination soar. We are thrilled to present you with a unique book featuring QR code technology.

Inside this book, you will find a variety of exciting activities. You can immerse yourself in the coloring pages. Explore the different sections: This book is divided into several exciting sections where you will find images of animals, flowers, fruits, and more.

Instructions:

You must have access to the internet and YouTube.

Each image contains a QR code that you can scan with your mobile camera. By scanning the code, you will be taken to a color version of the image on your screen, and in most cases, you can also enjoy a sound related to the image. It's as if the pages come to life!

Have fun exploring the coloring sections and discover the magic of QR codes!

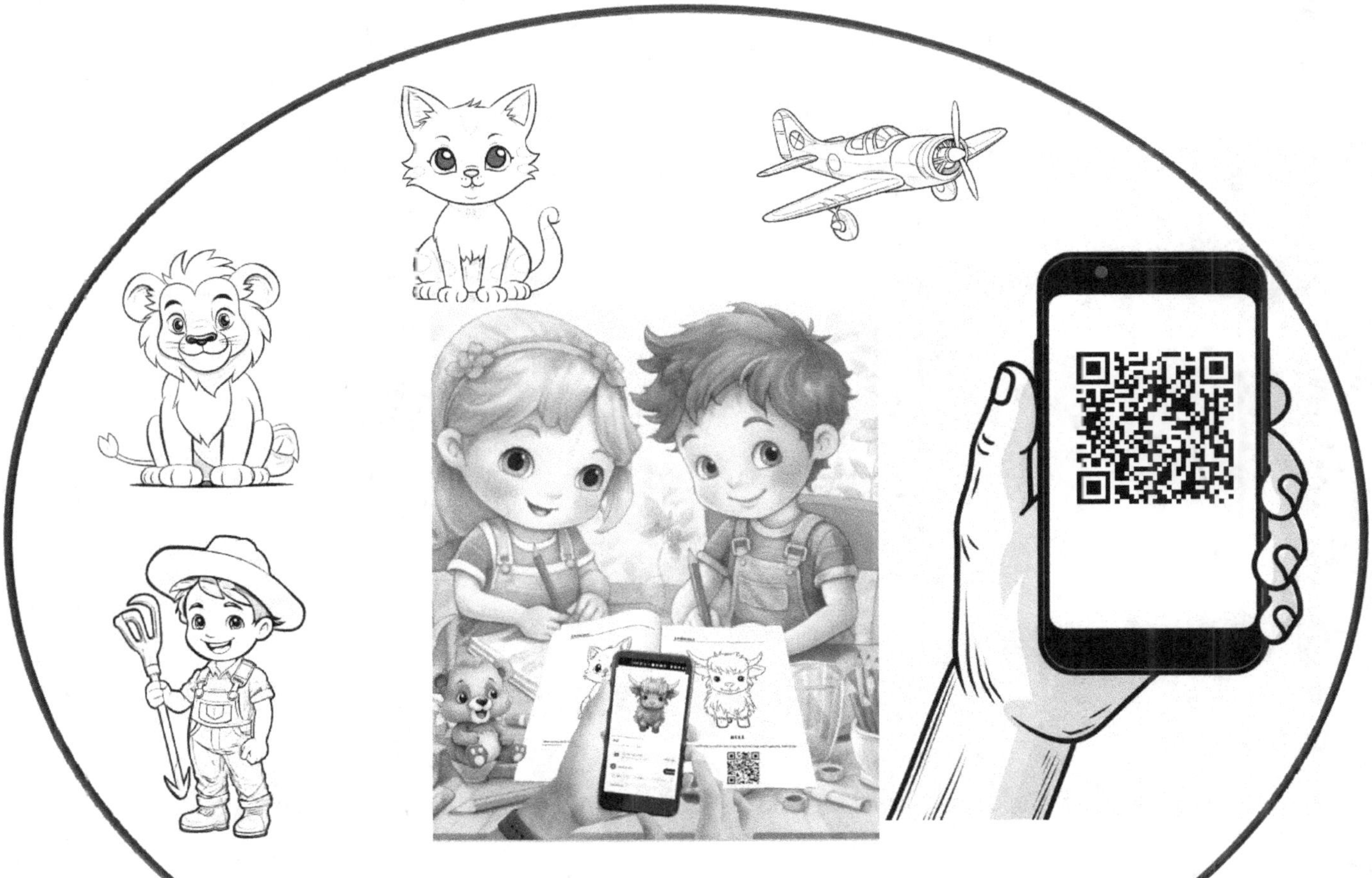

ANIMALS

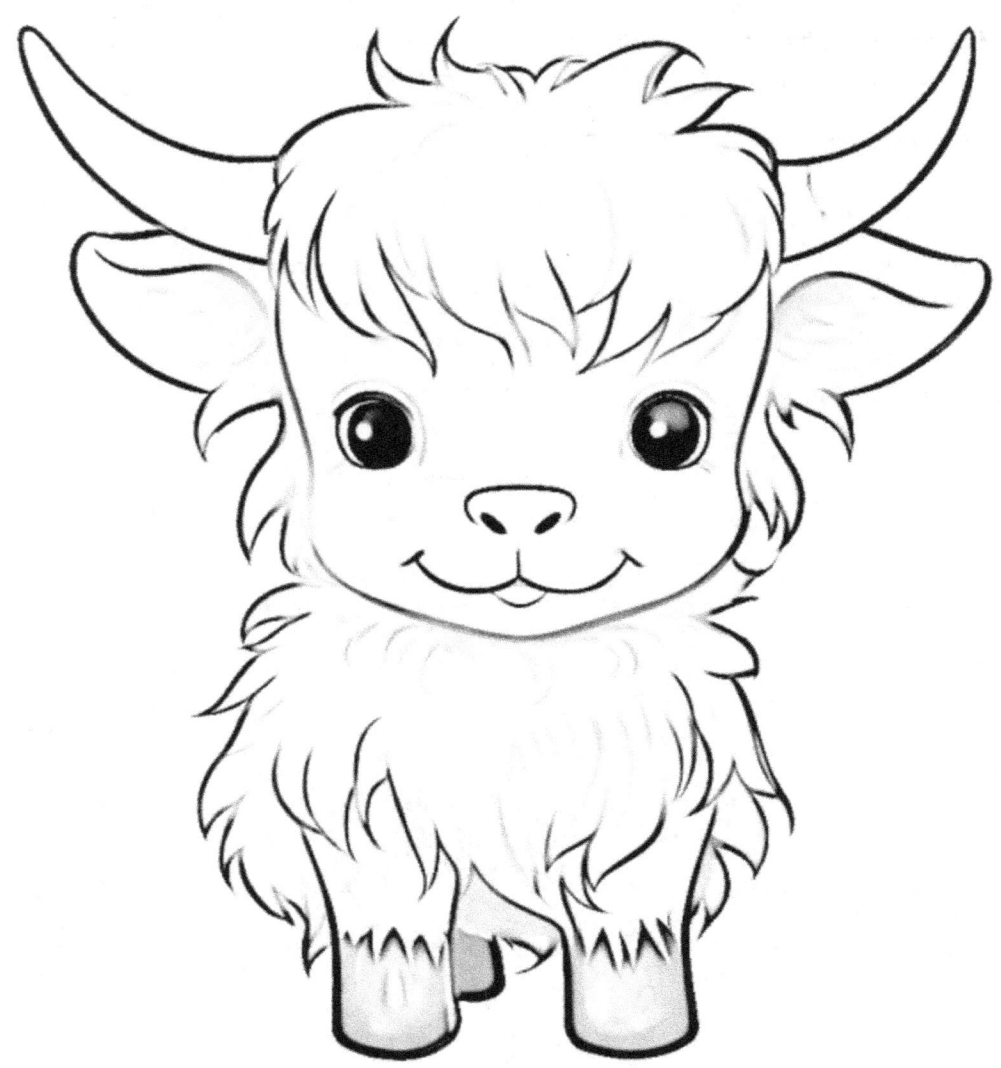

BULL

When scanning the QR code, you will be able to see the colored image and, if applicable, listen to the associated sound.

ANATOMY

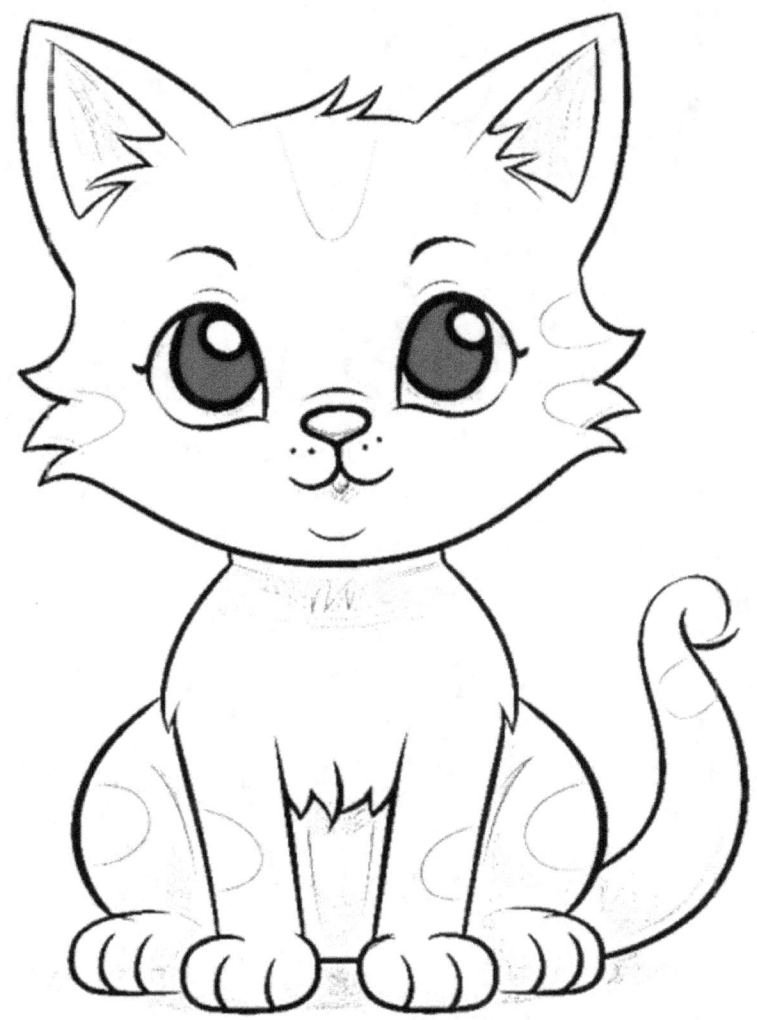

CAT

When scanning the QR code, you will be able to see the colored image and, if applicable, listen to the associated sound.

ANIMALS

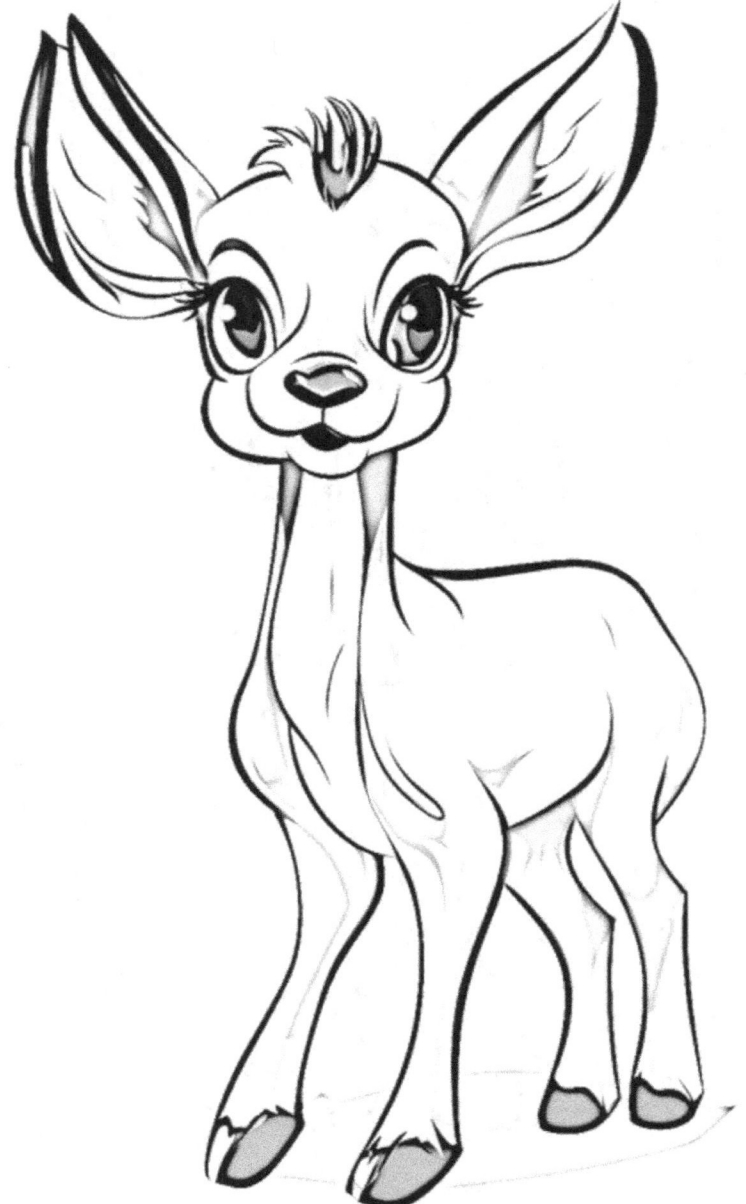

ANTELOPE

When scanning the QR code, you will be able to see the colored image and, if applicable, listen to the associated sound.

ANIMALS

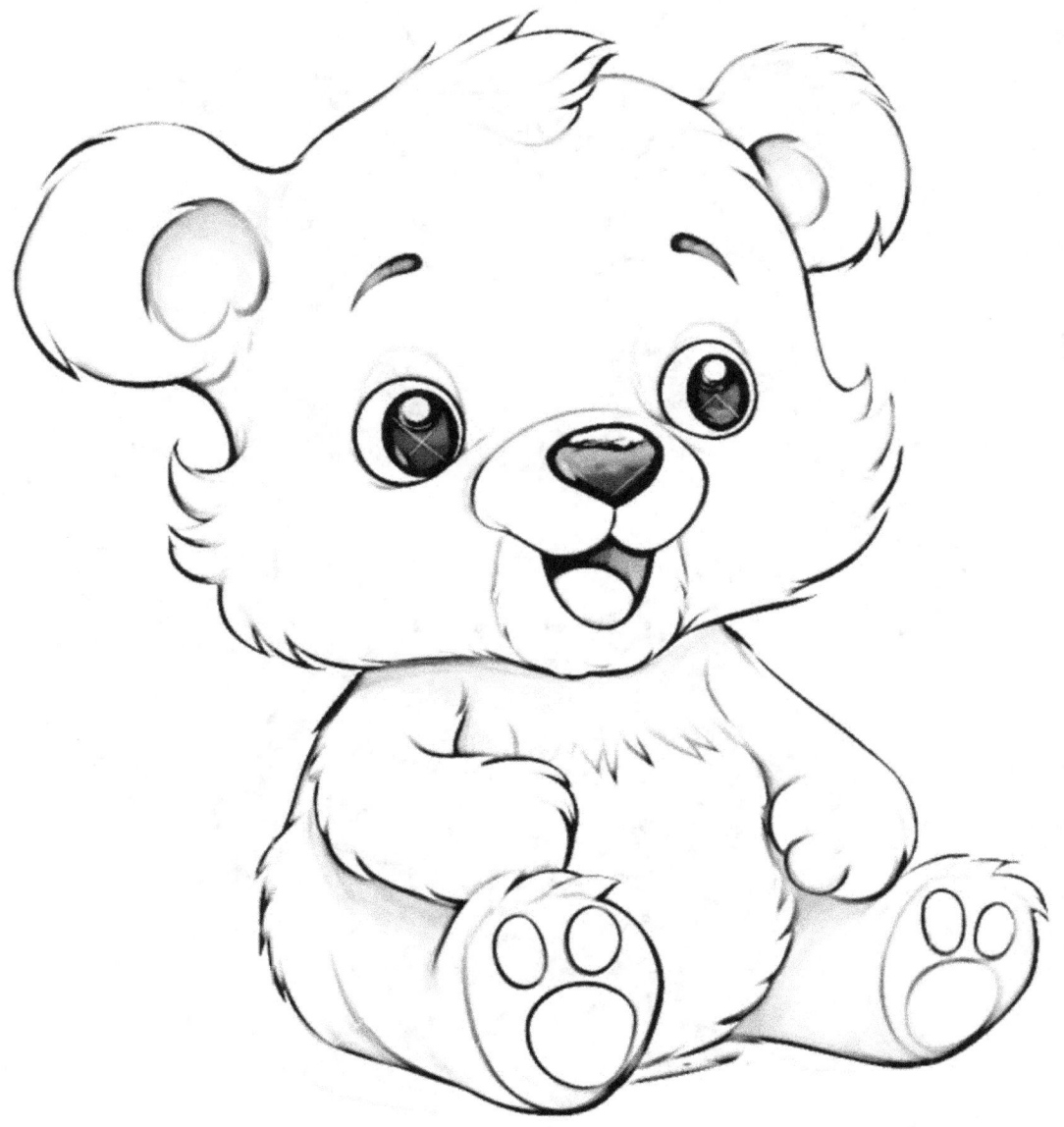

BEAR

When scanning the QR code, you will be able to see the colored image and, if applicable, listen to the associated sound.

ANANIMALS

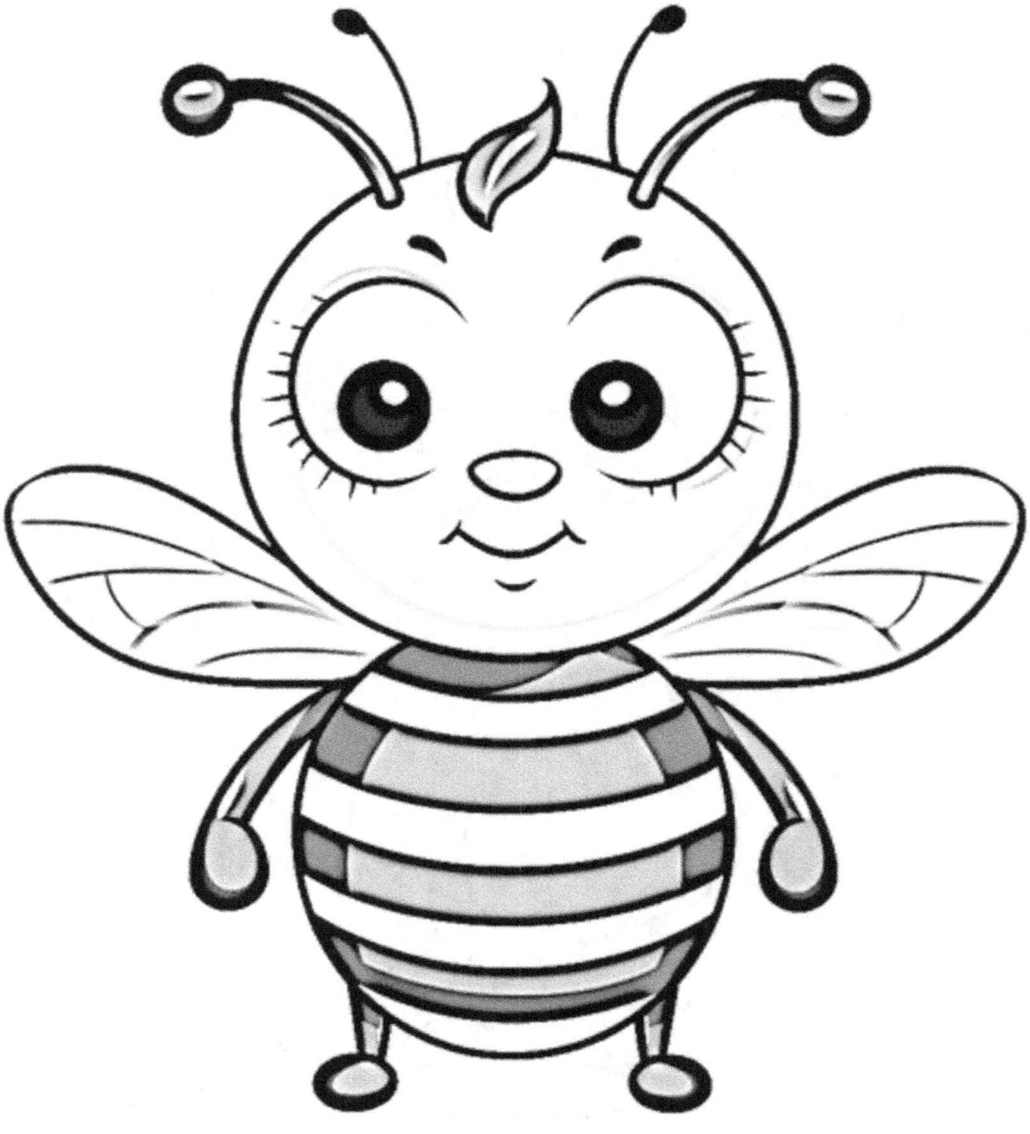

BEE

When scanning the QR code, you will be able to see the colored image and, if applicable, listen to the associated sound.

ANIMALS

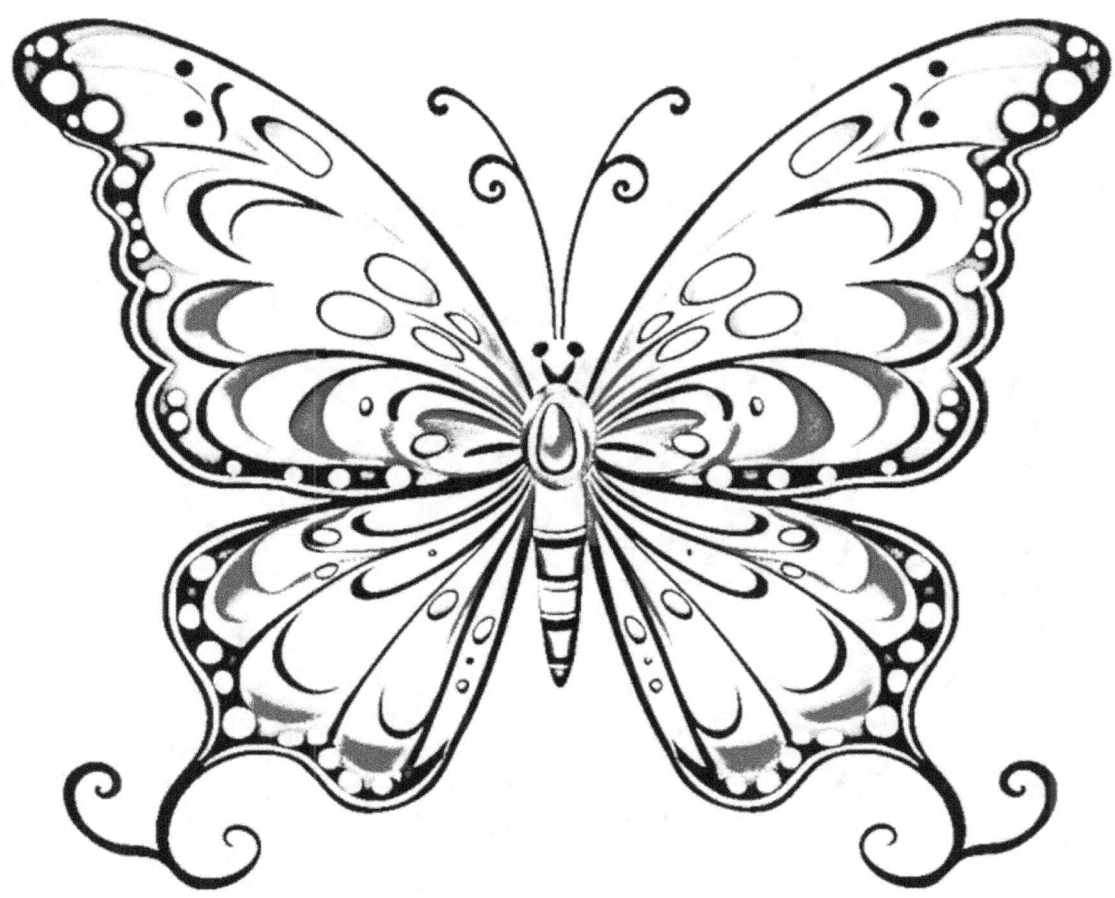

BUTTEFLY

When scanning the QR code, you will be able to see the colored image and, if applicable, listen to the associated scund.

ANALS

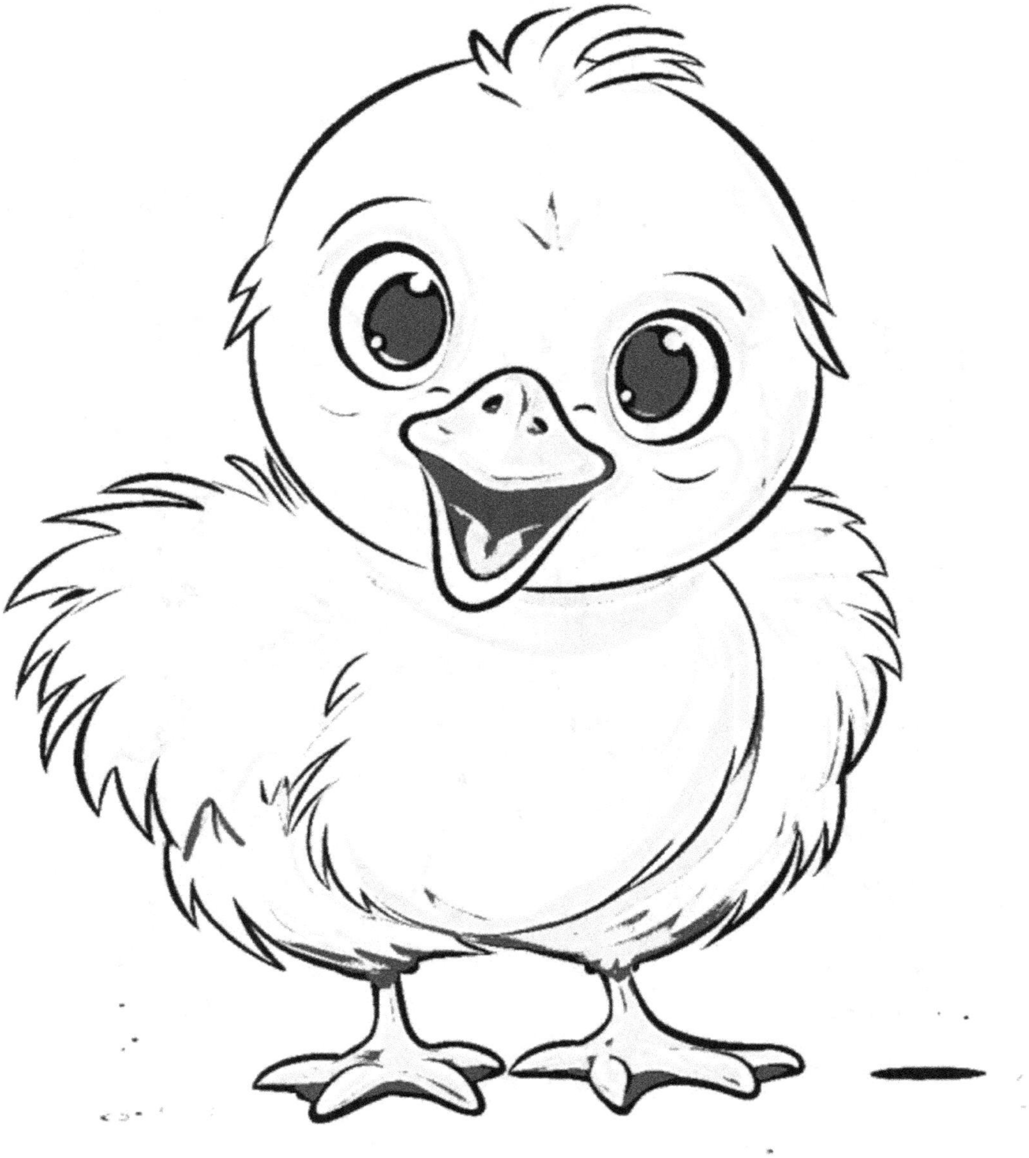

CHICKEN

When scanning the QR code, you will be able to see the colored image and, if applicable, listen to the associated sound.

ANIMALS

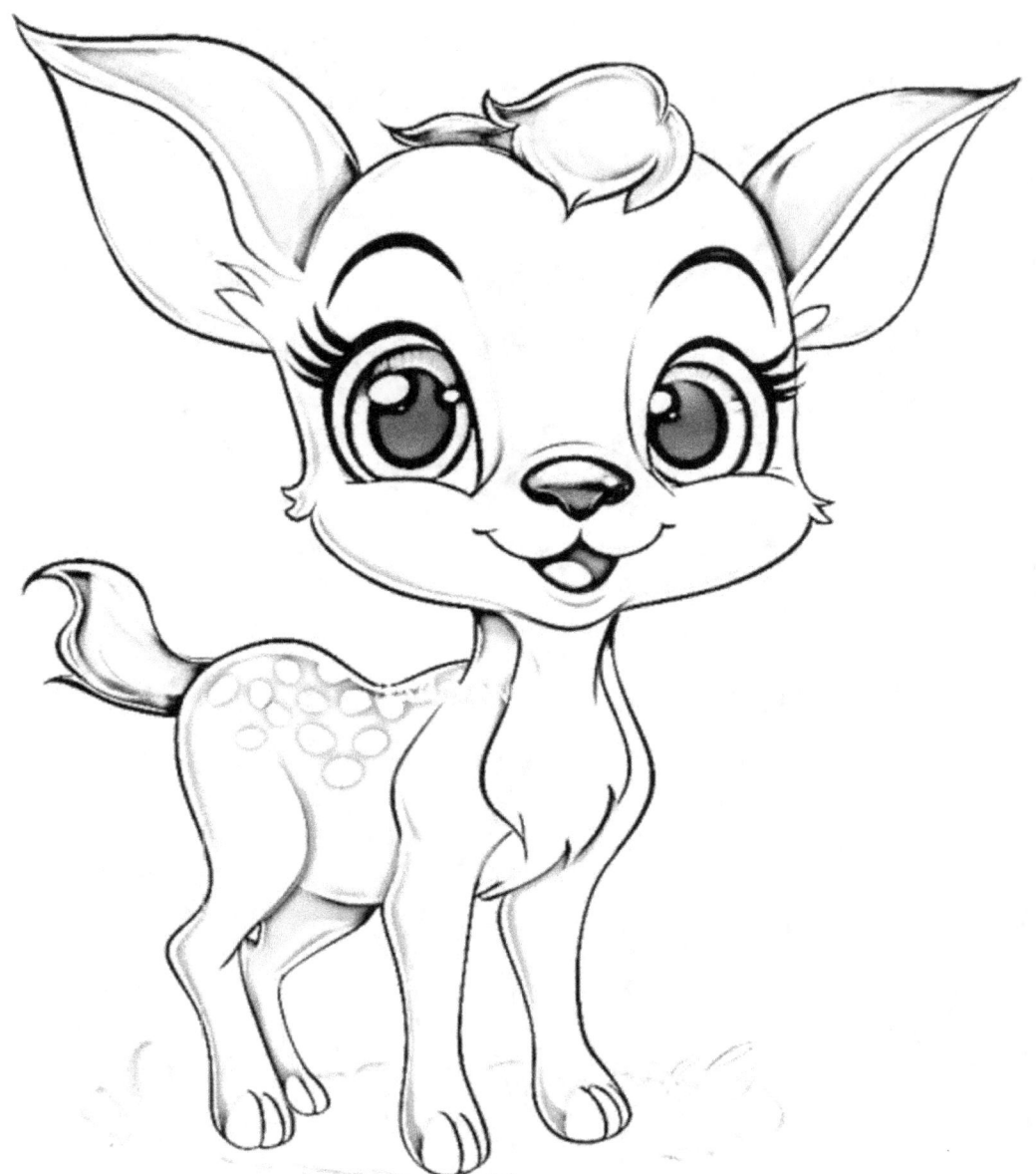

ANTELOPE

When scanning the QR code, you will be able to see the colored image and, if applicable, listen to the associated sound.

ANIMALS

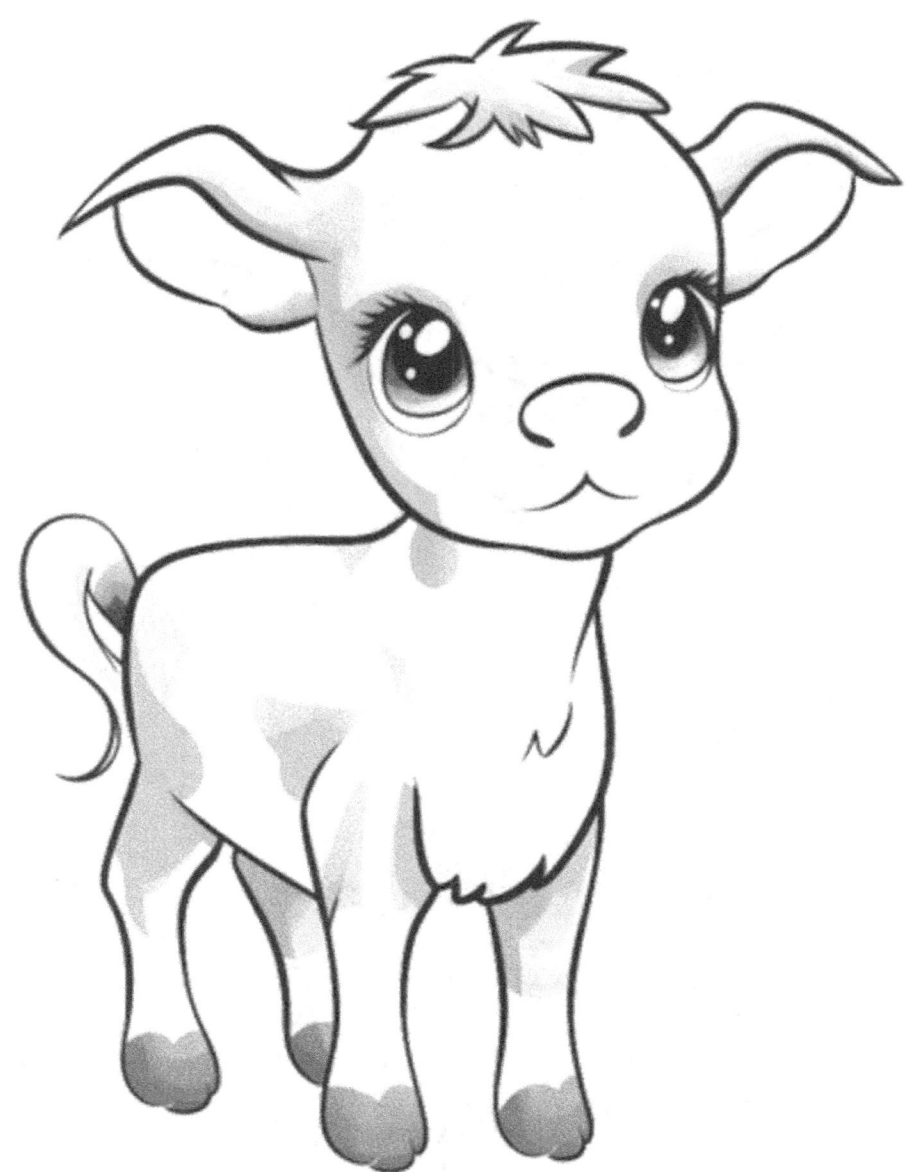

COW

.When scanning the QR code, you will be able to see the colored image and, if applicable, listen to the associated sound

ANIMALS

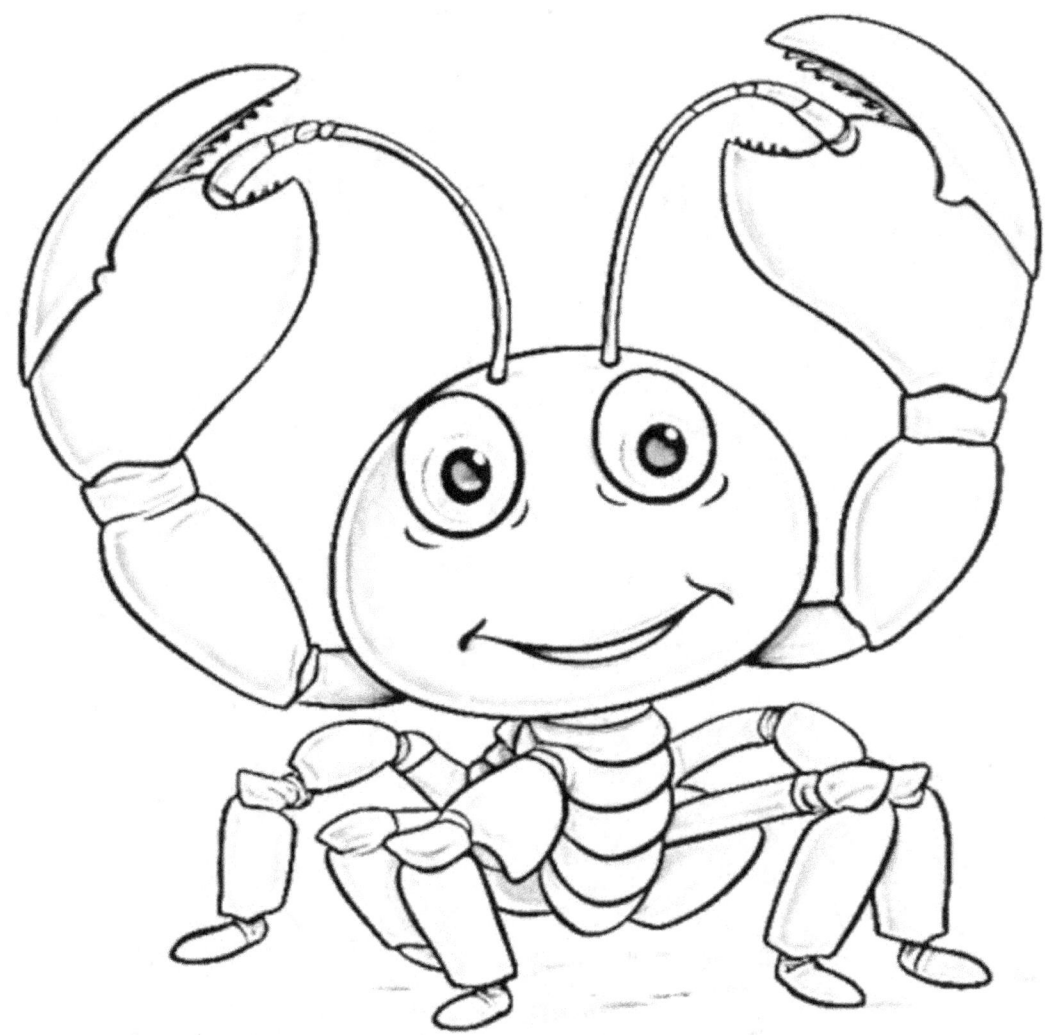

GRAB

When scanning the QR code, you will be able to see the colored image and, if applicable, listen to the associated sound.

ANIMALS

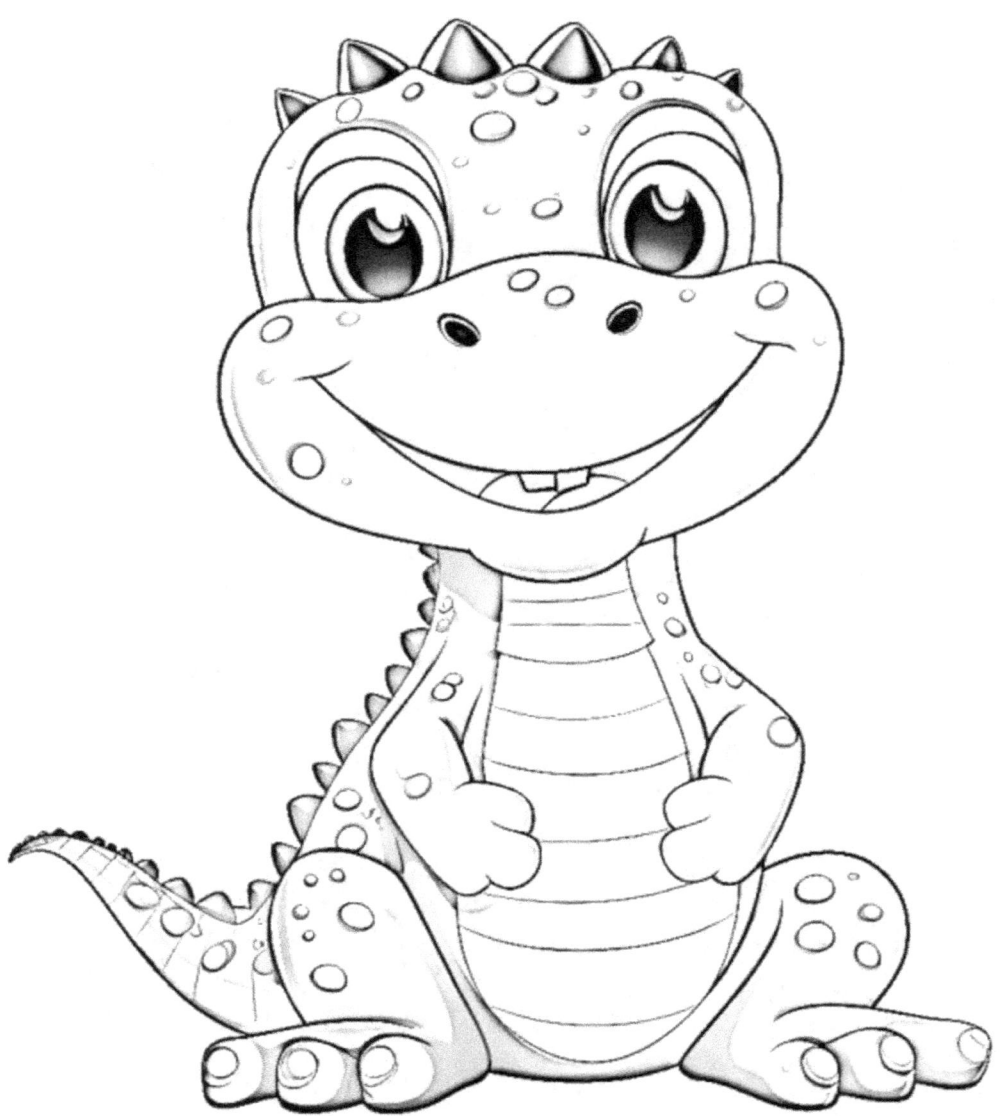

CROCODILE

When scanning the QR code, you will be able to see the colored image and, if applicable, listen to the associated sound.

ANIMALS

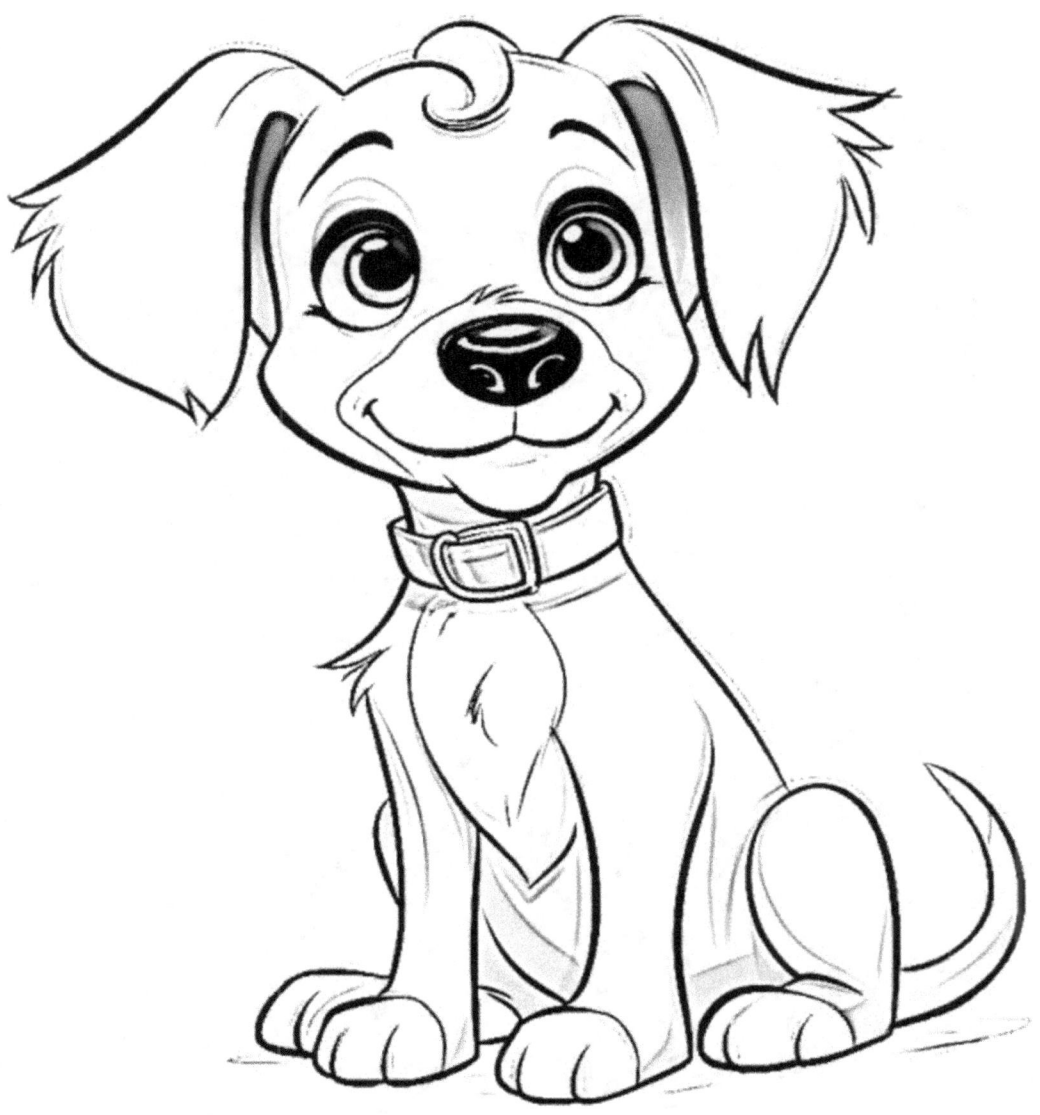

DOG

When scanning the QR code, you will be able to see the colored image and, if applicable, listen to the associated sound.

ANALS

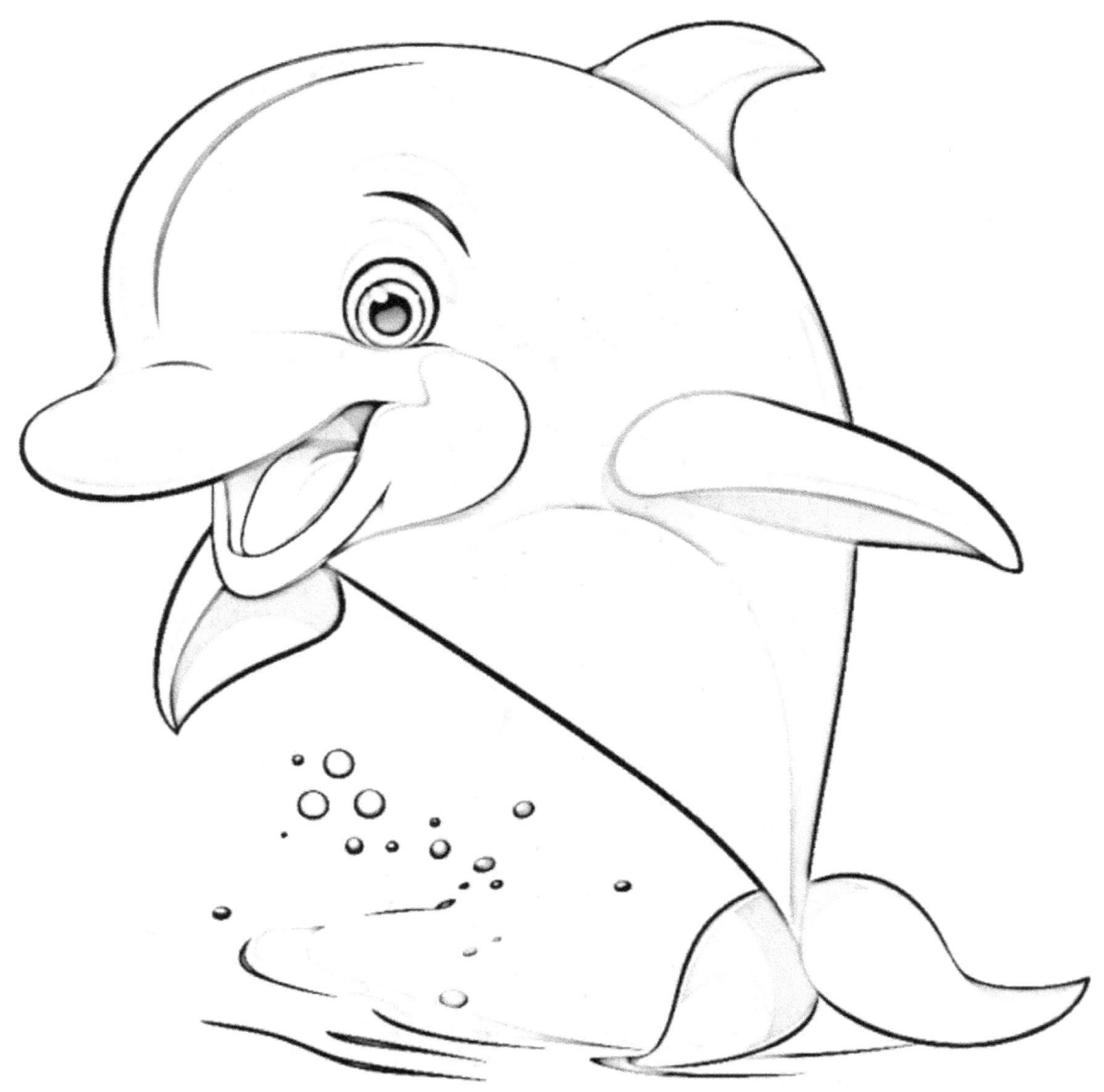

DOLPHIN

When scanning the QR code, you will be able to see the colored image and, if applicable, listen to the associated sound.

ANIMALS

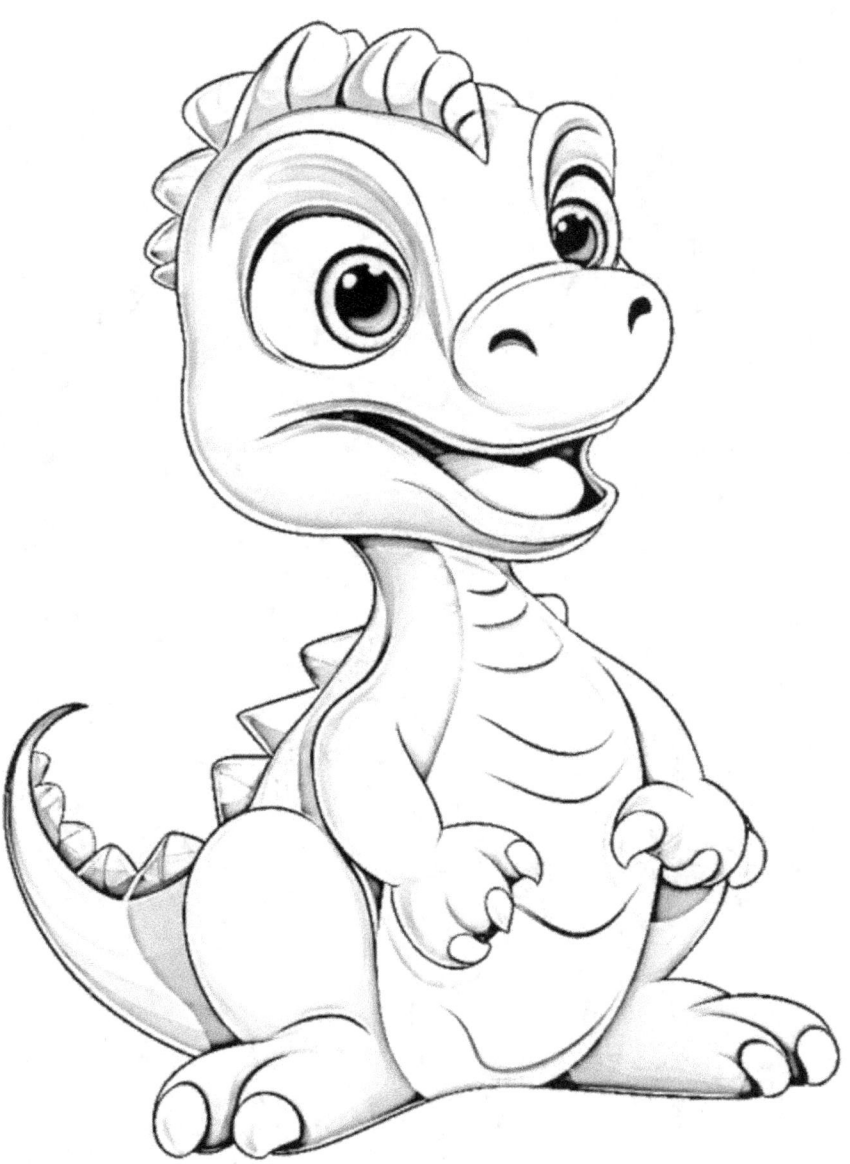

DINOSAUR

When scanning the QR code, you will be able to see the colored image and, if applicable, listen to the associated sound.

ANIMALS

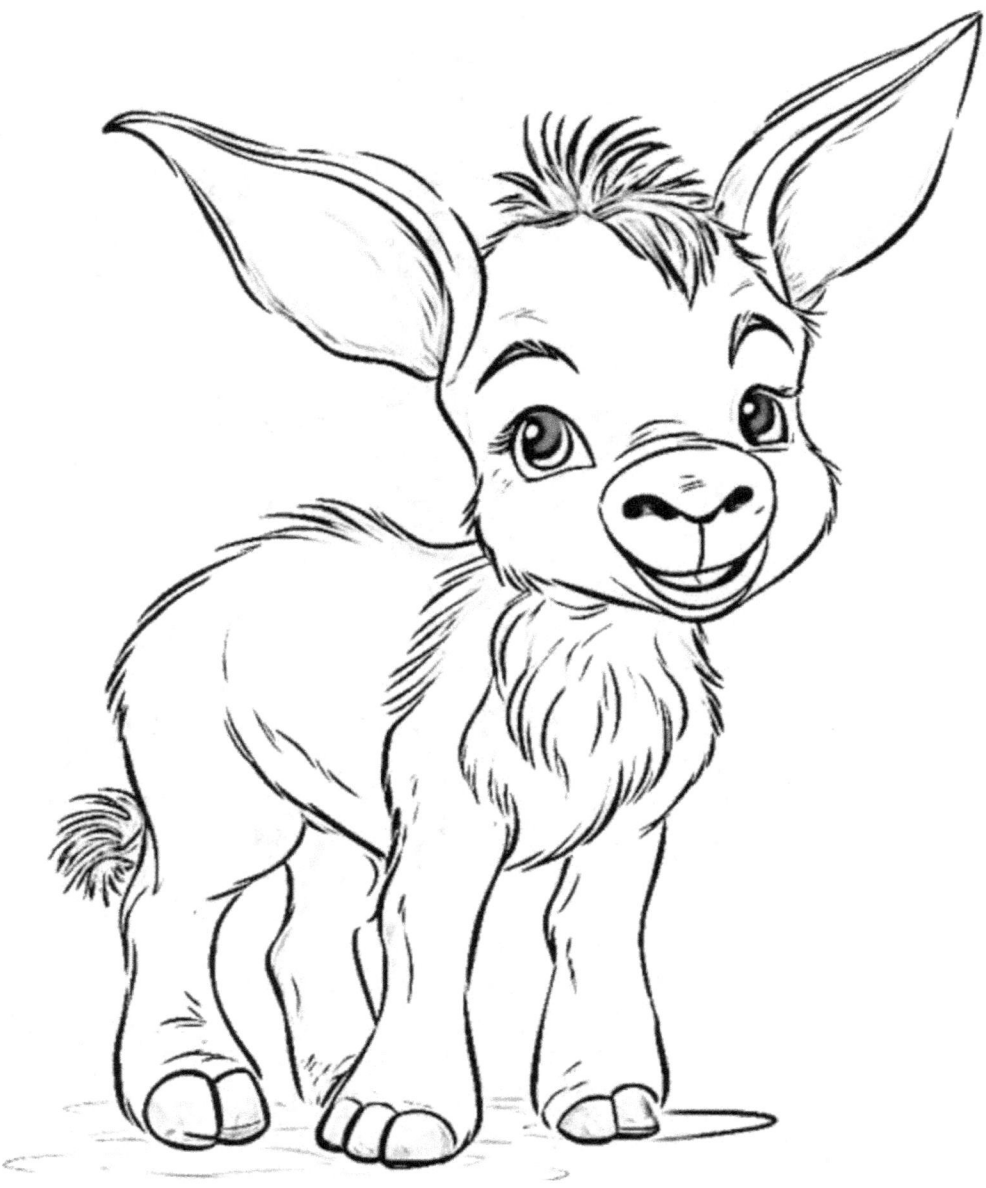

DONKEY

When scanning the QR code, you will be able to see the colored image and, if applicable, listen to the associated sound.

ANINALS

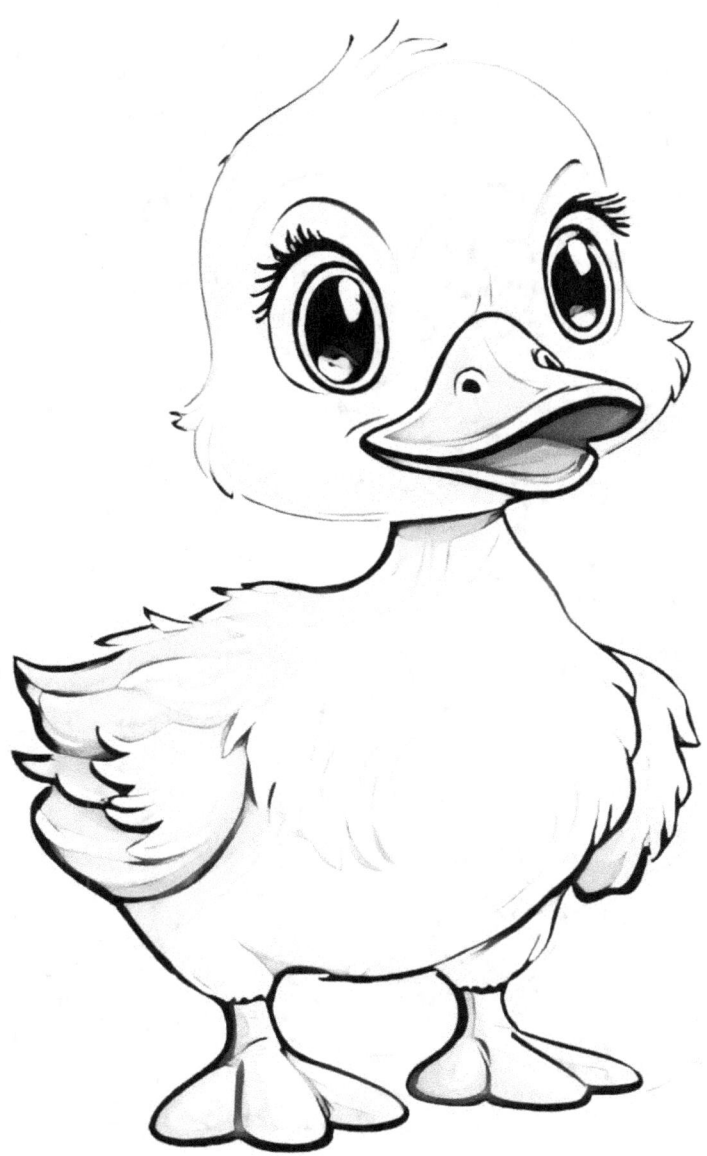

DUCK

When scanning the QR code, you will be able to see the colored image and, if applicable, listen to the associated sound.

ANANIMALS

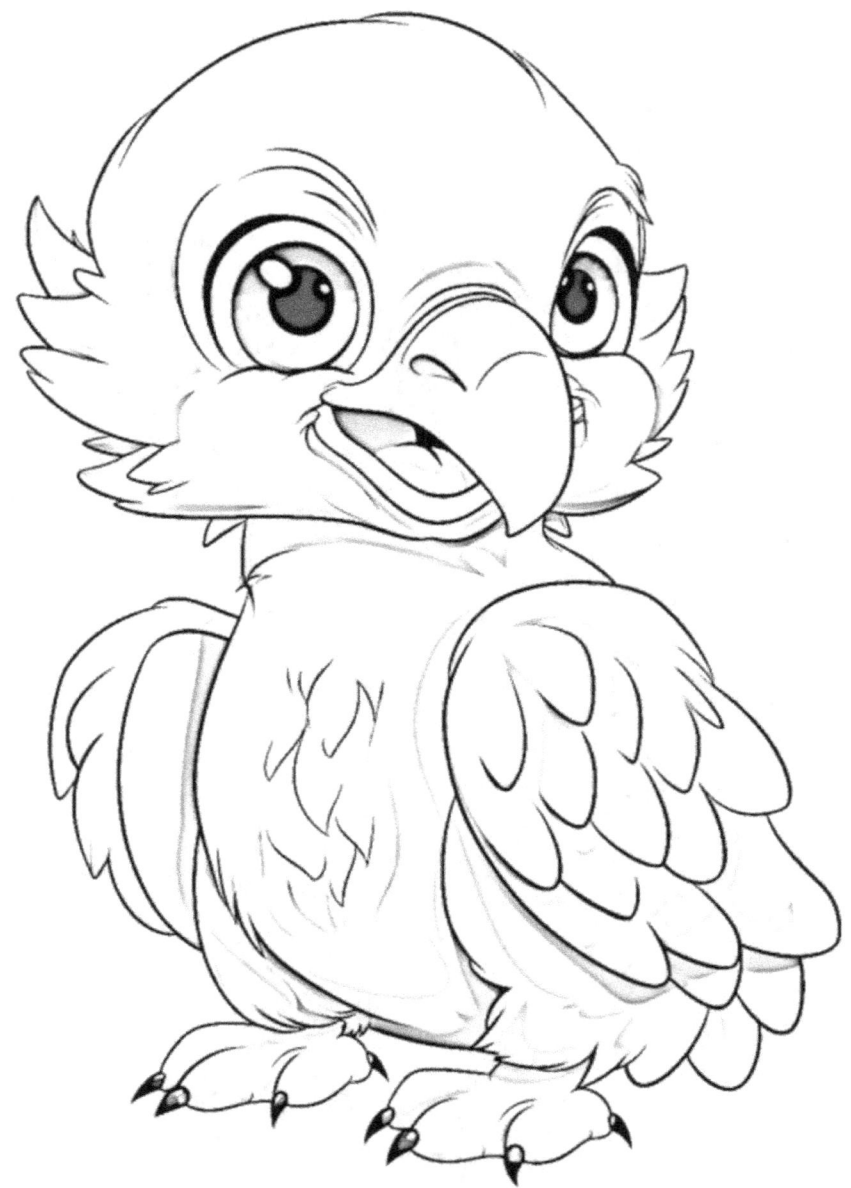

EAGLE

When scanning the QR code, you will be able to see the colored image and, if applicable, listen to the associated sound.

ANIMALS

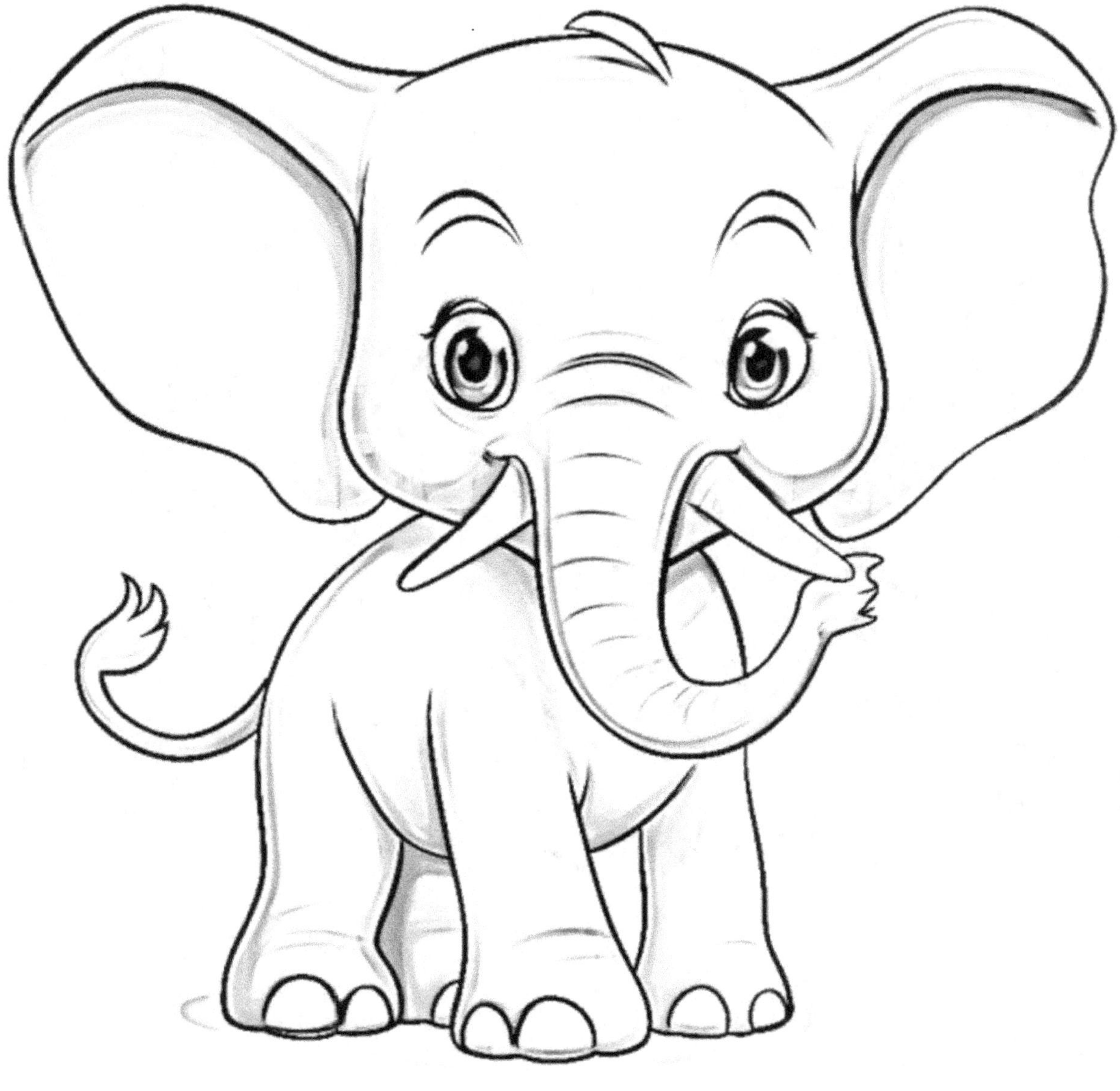

ELEPHANT

When scanning the QR code, you will be able to see the colored image and, if applicable, listen to the associated sound.

ANIMALS

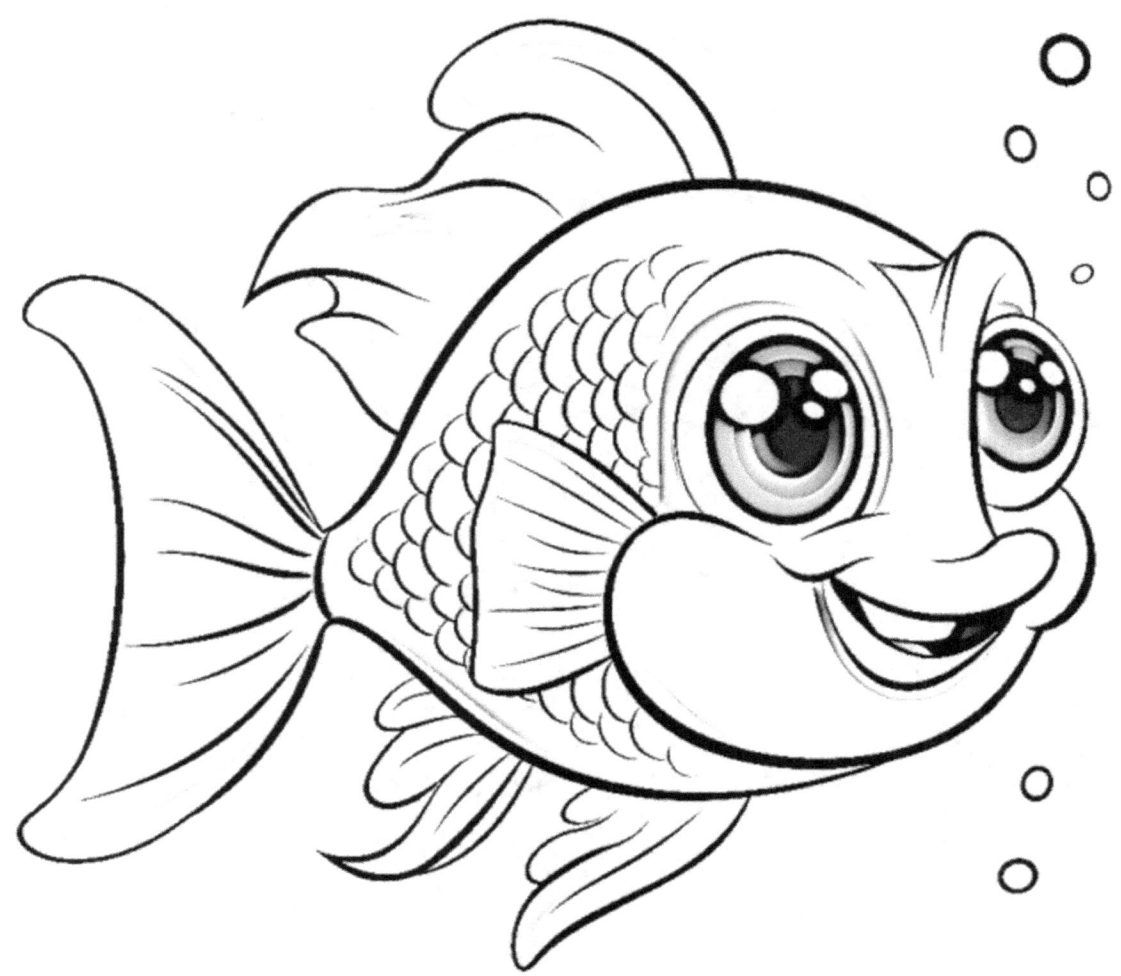

FISH

When scanning the QR code, you will be able to see the colored image and, if applicable, listen to the associated sound.

ANIMALS

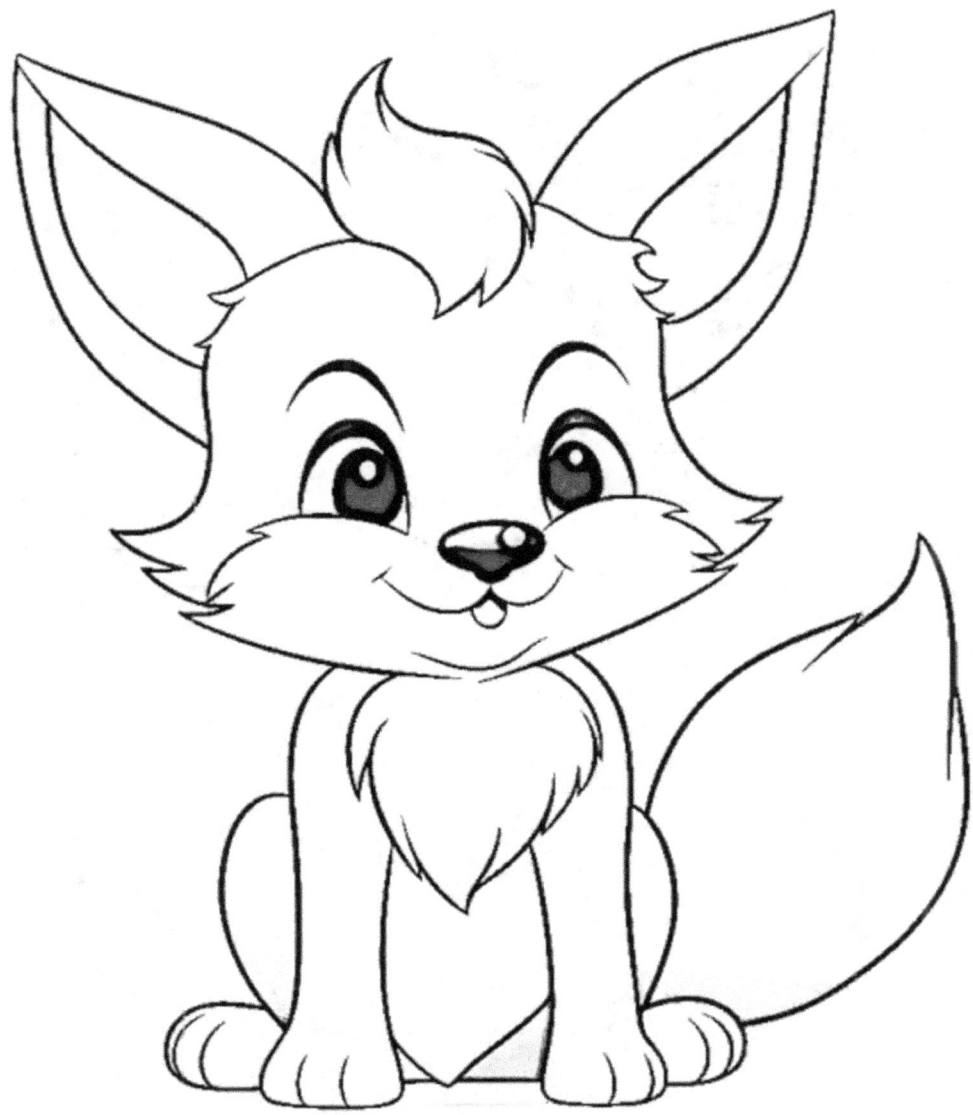

FOX

When scanning the QR code, you will be able to see the colored image and, if applicable, listen to the associated sound.

ANIMALS

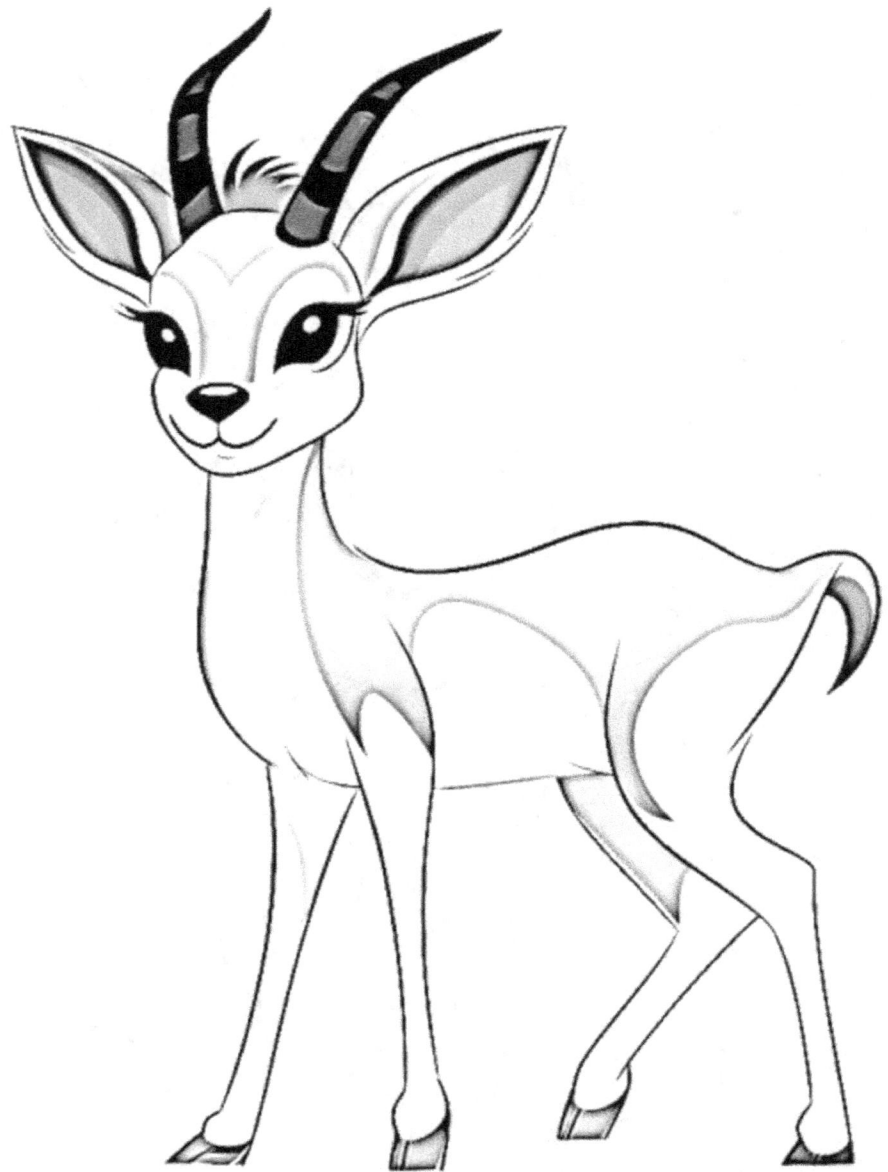

GAZELLE

When scanning the QR code, you will be able to see the colored image and, if applicable, listen to the associated sound.

ANIMALS

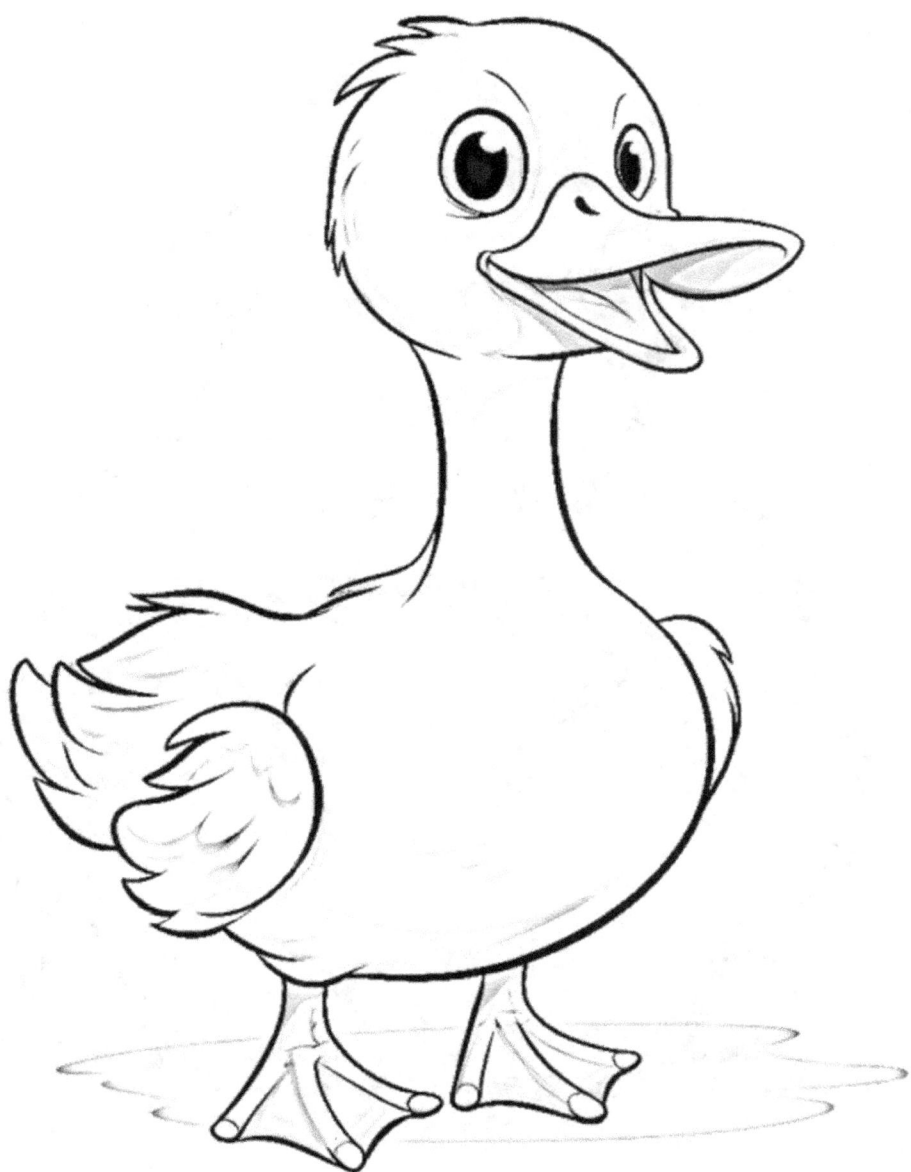

GOOSE

When scanning the QR code, you will be able to see the colored image and, if applicable, listen to the associated sound.

ANIMALS

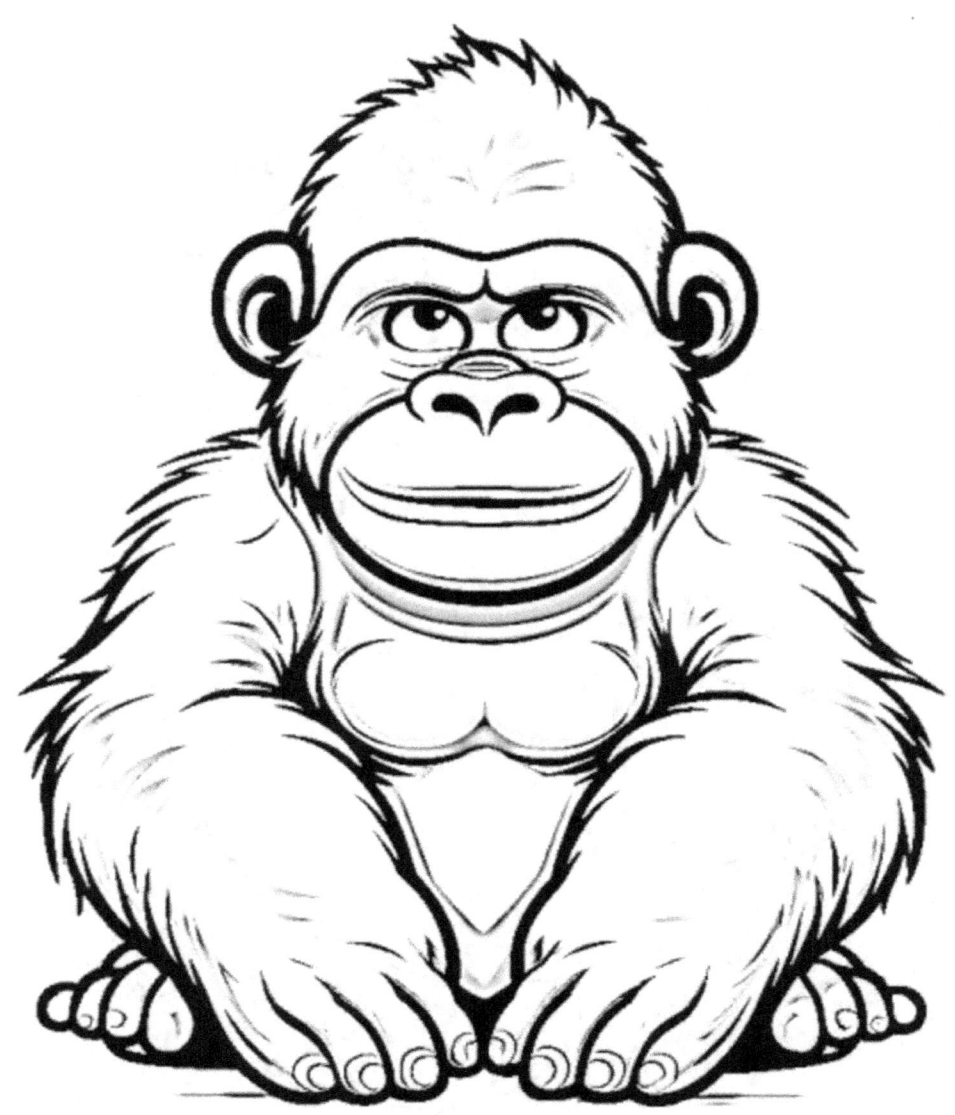

GORILLA

When scanning the QR code, you will be able to see the colored image and, if applicable, listen to the associated sound.

ANALS

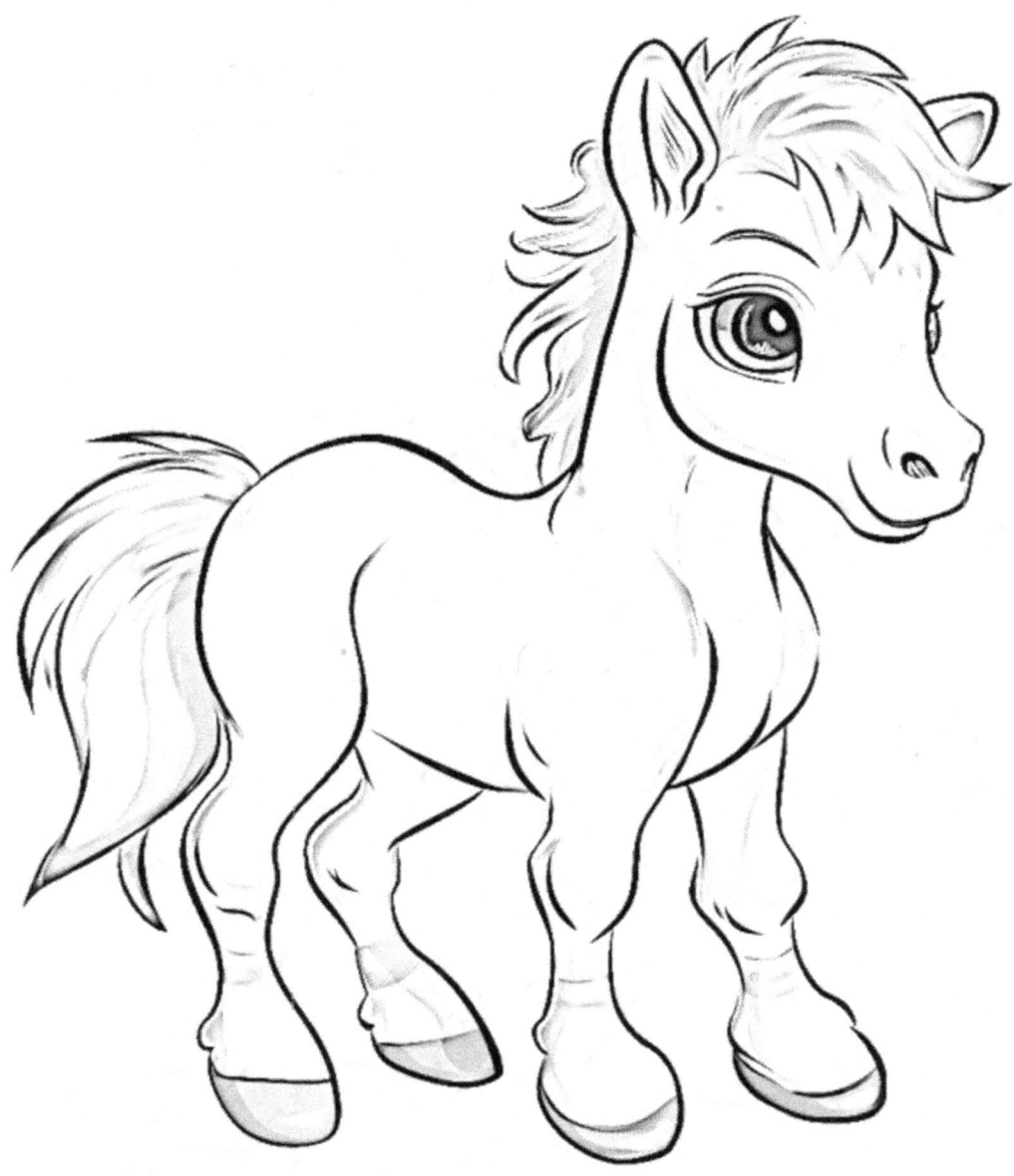

HORSE

When scanning the QR code, you will be able to see the colored image and, if applicable, listen to the associated sound.

ANIMALS

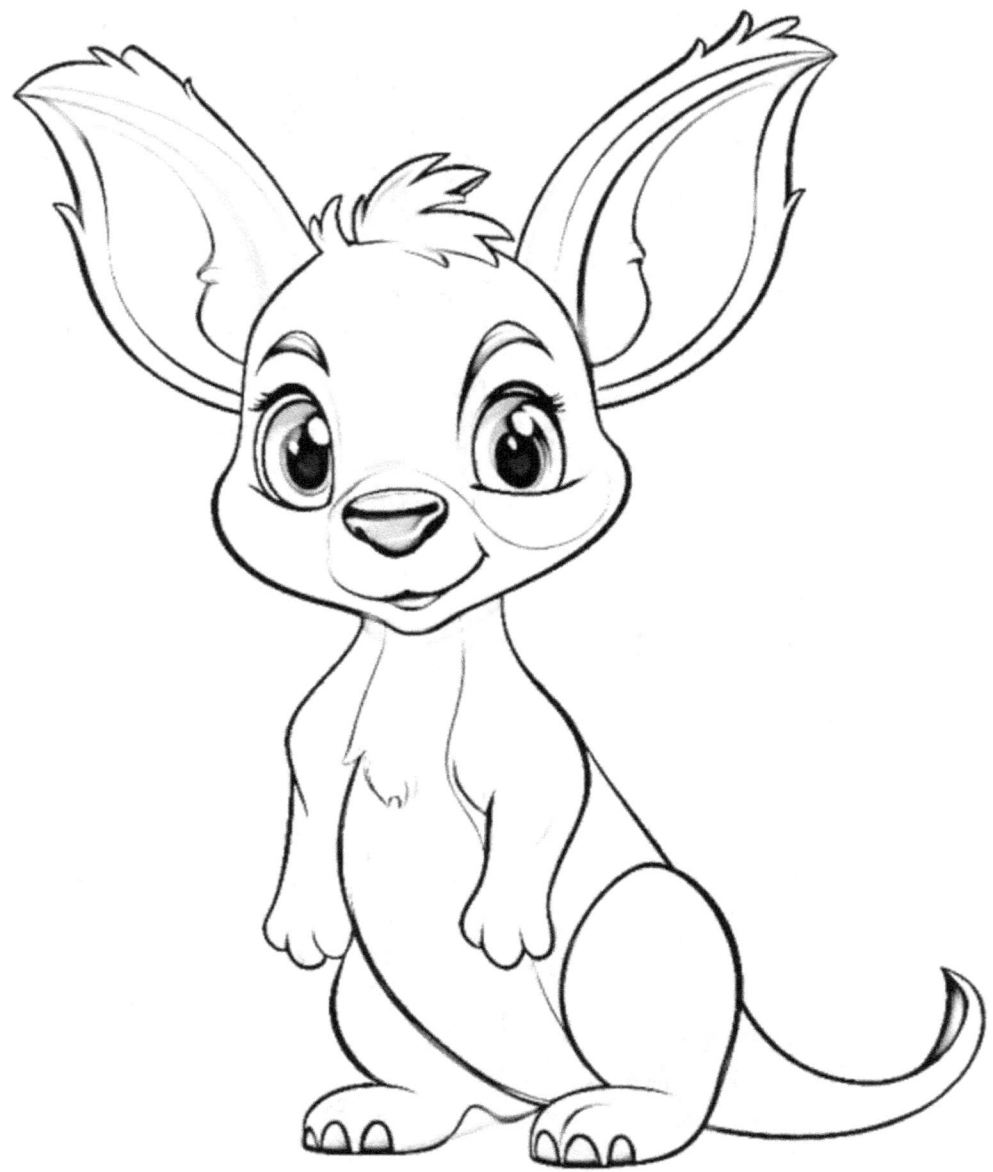

KANGAROO

When scanning the QR code, you will be able to see the colored image and, if applicable, listen to the associated sound.

ANIMALS

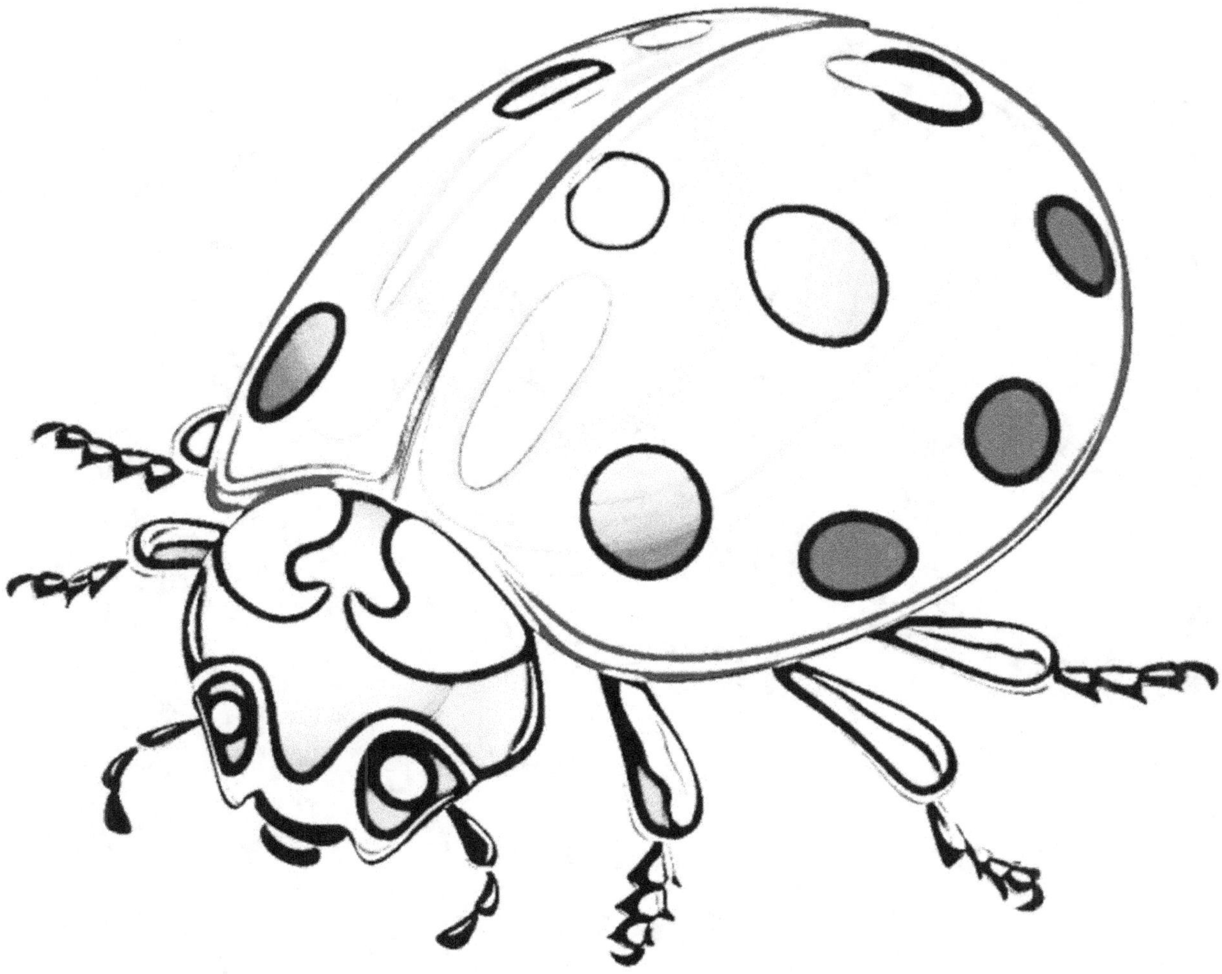

LADYBUG

When scanning the QR code, you will be able to see the colored image and, if applicable, listen to the associated sound.

ANIMALS

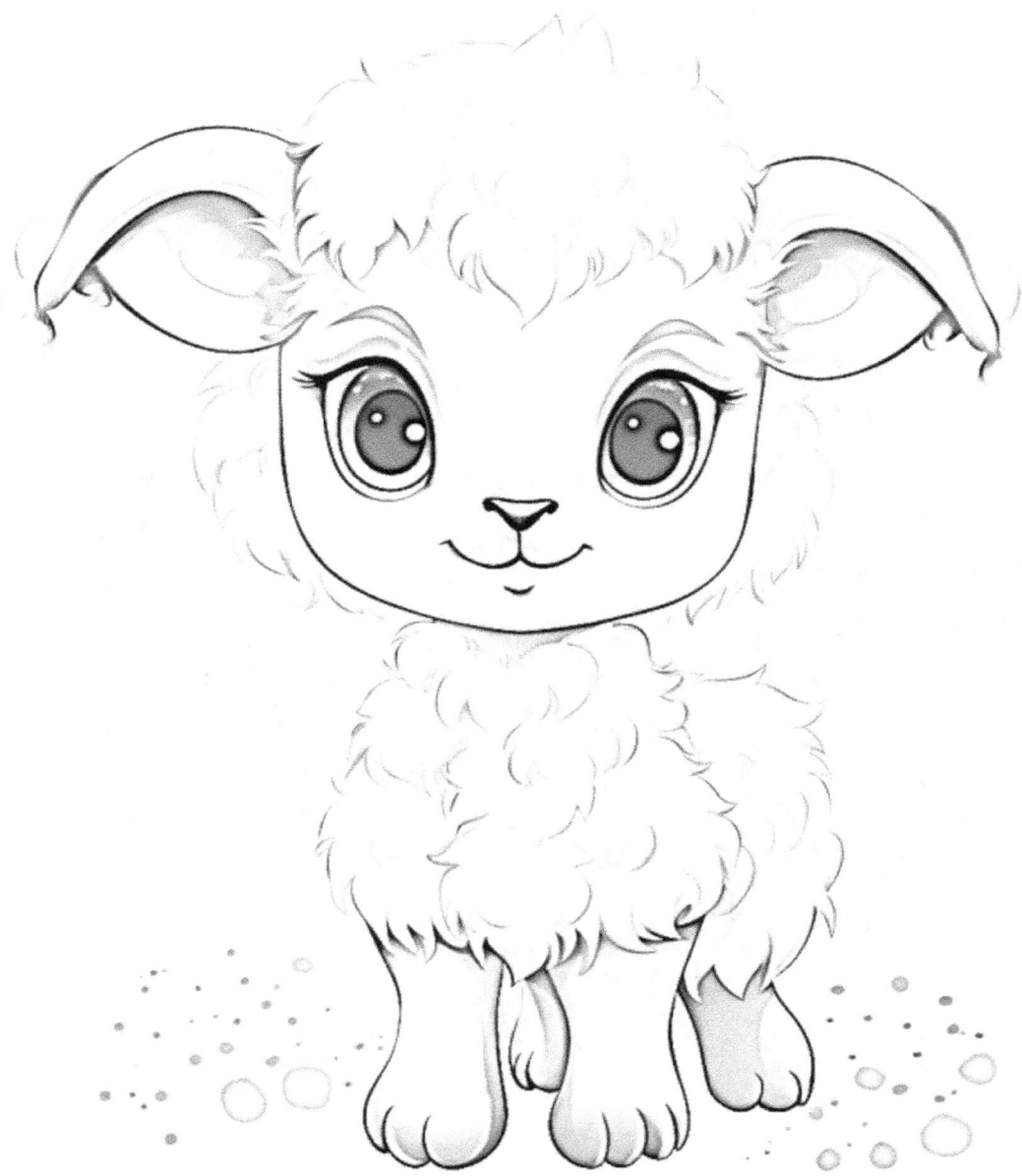

LAMB

When scanning the QR code, you will be able to see the colored image and, if applicable, listen to the associated sound.

ANIMALS

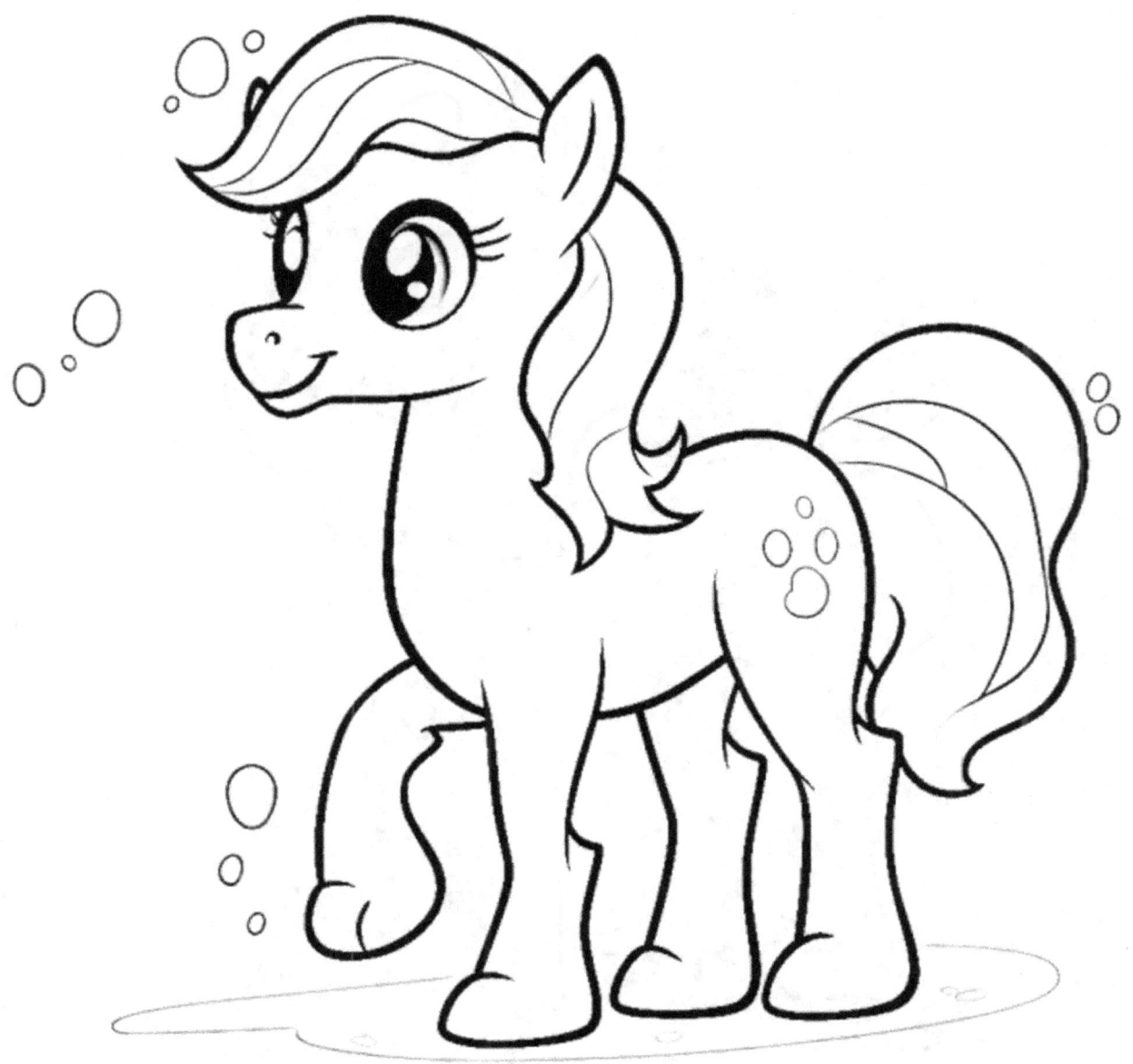

HORSE

When scanning the QR code, you will be able to see the colored image and, if applicable, listen to the associated sound.

ANIMALS

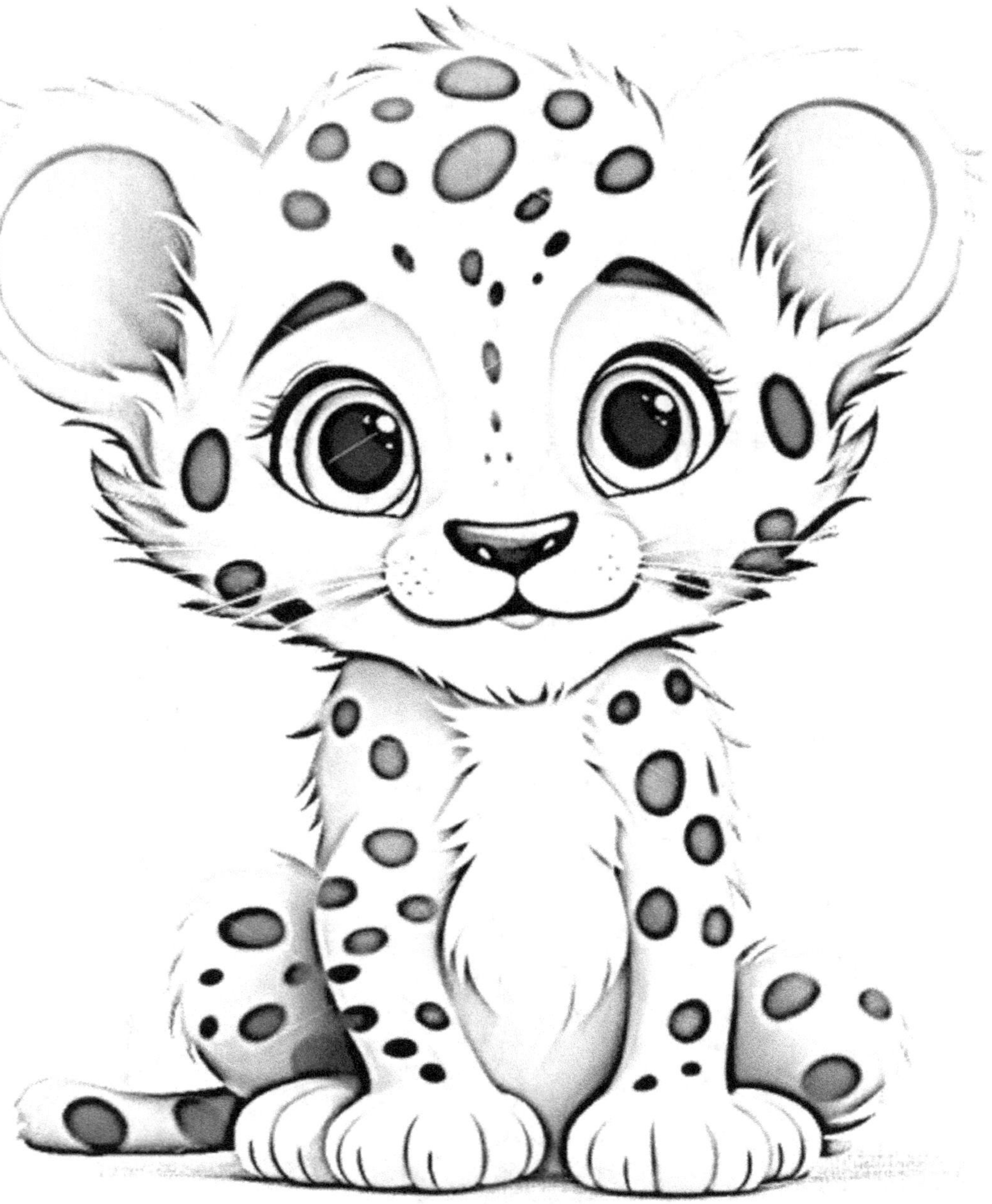

LEOPARD

When scanning the QR code, you will be able to see the colored image and, if applicable, listen to the associated sound.

ANIMALS

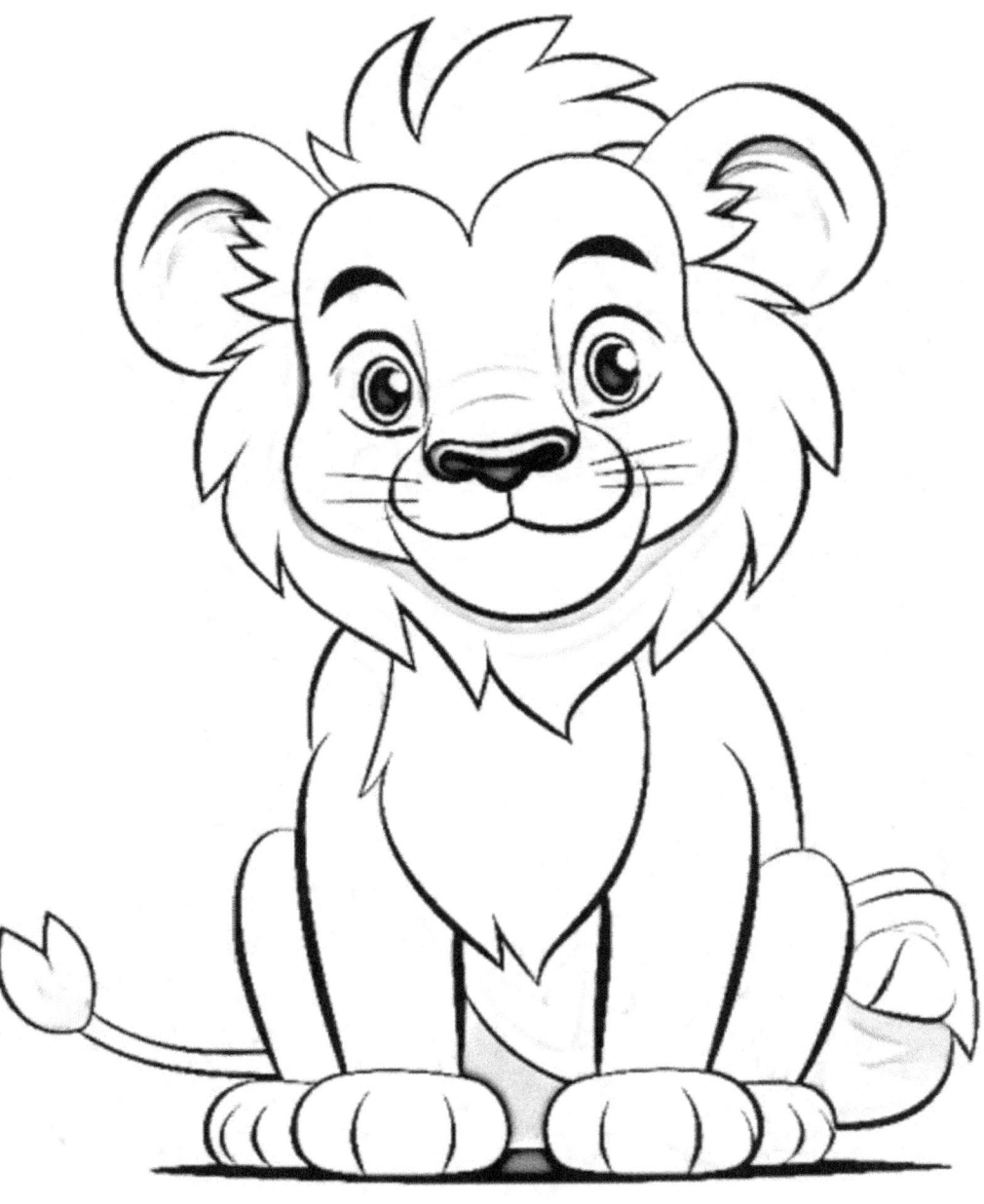

LION

When scanning the QR code, you will be able to see the colored image and, if applicable, listen to the associated sound.

ANIMALS

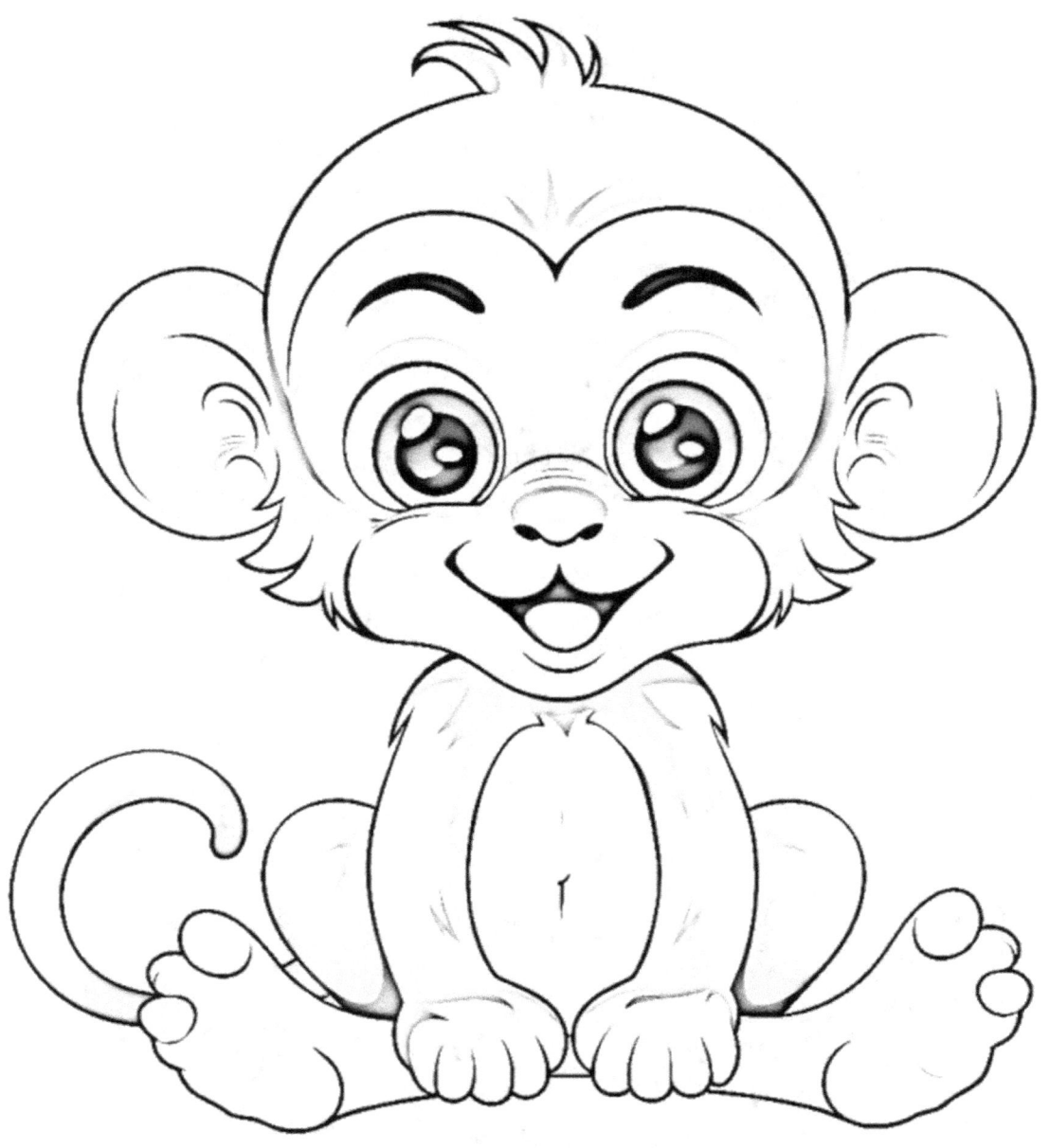

MONKY

When scanning the QR code, you will be able to see the colored image and, if applicable, listen to the associated sound.

ANIMALS

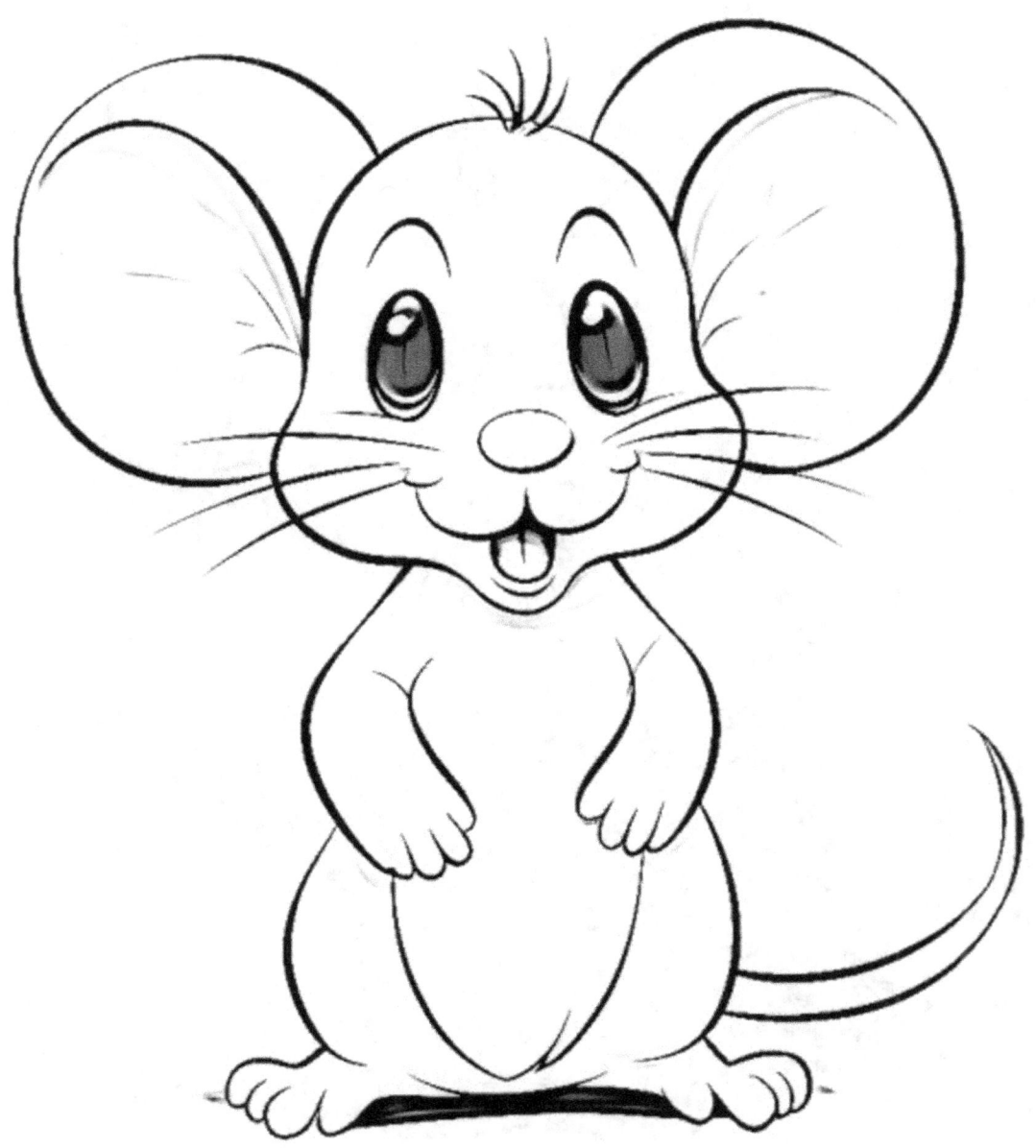

MOUSE

When scanning the QR code, you will be able to see the colored image and, if applicable, listen to the associated sound.

ANIMALS

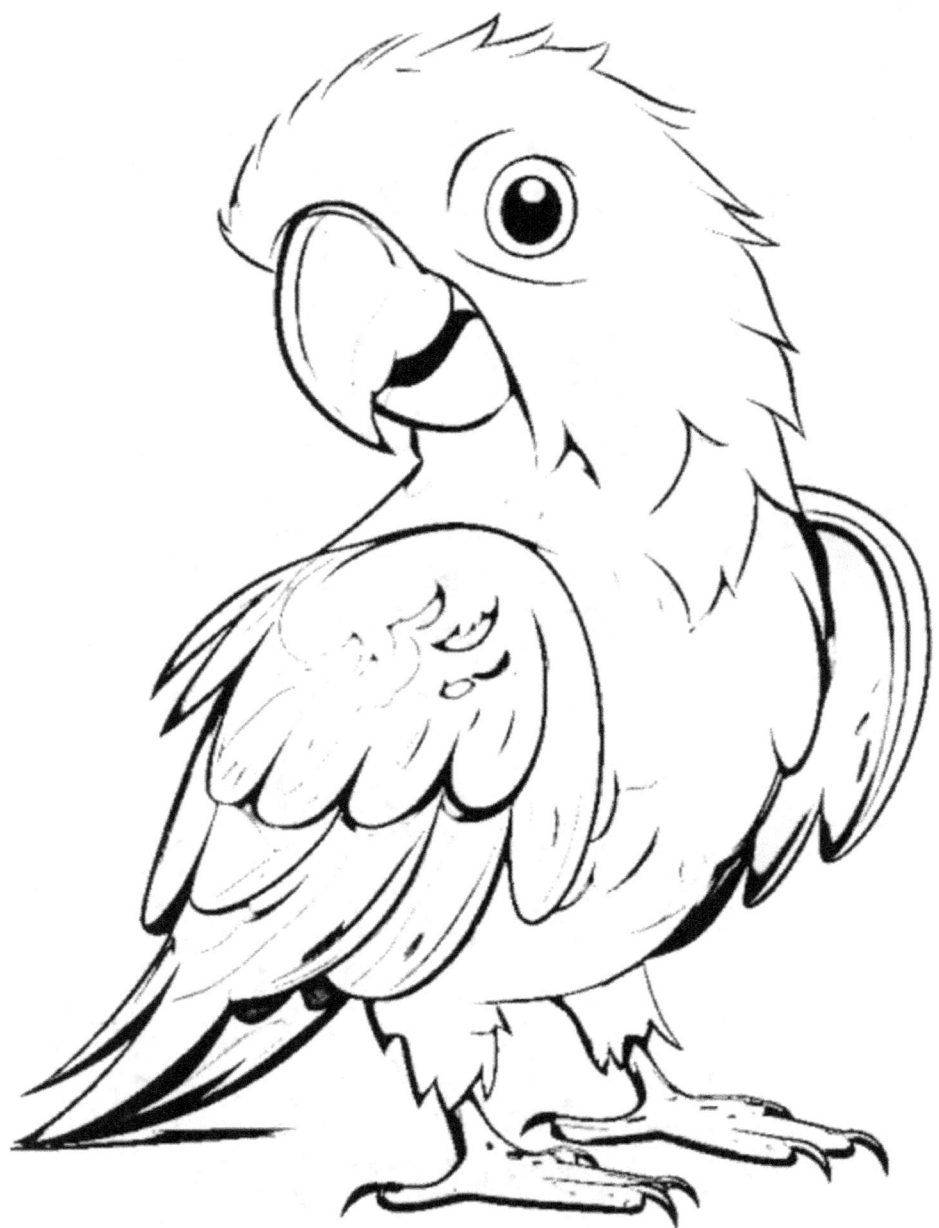

PARROT

When scanning the QR code, you will be able to see the colored image and, if applicable, listen to the associated sound.

ANIMALS

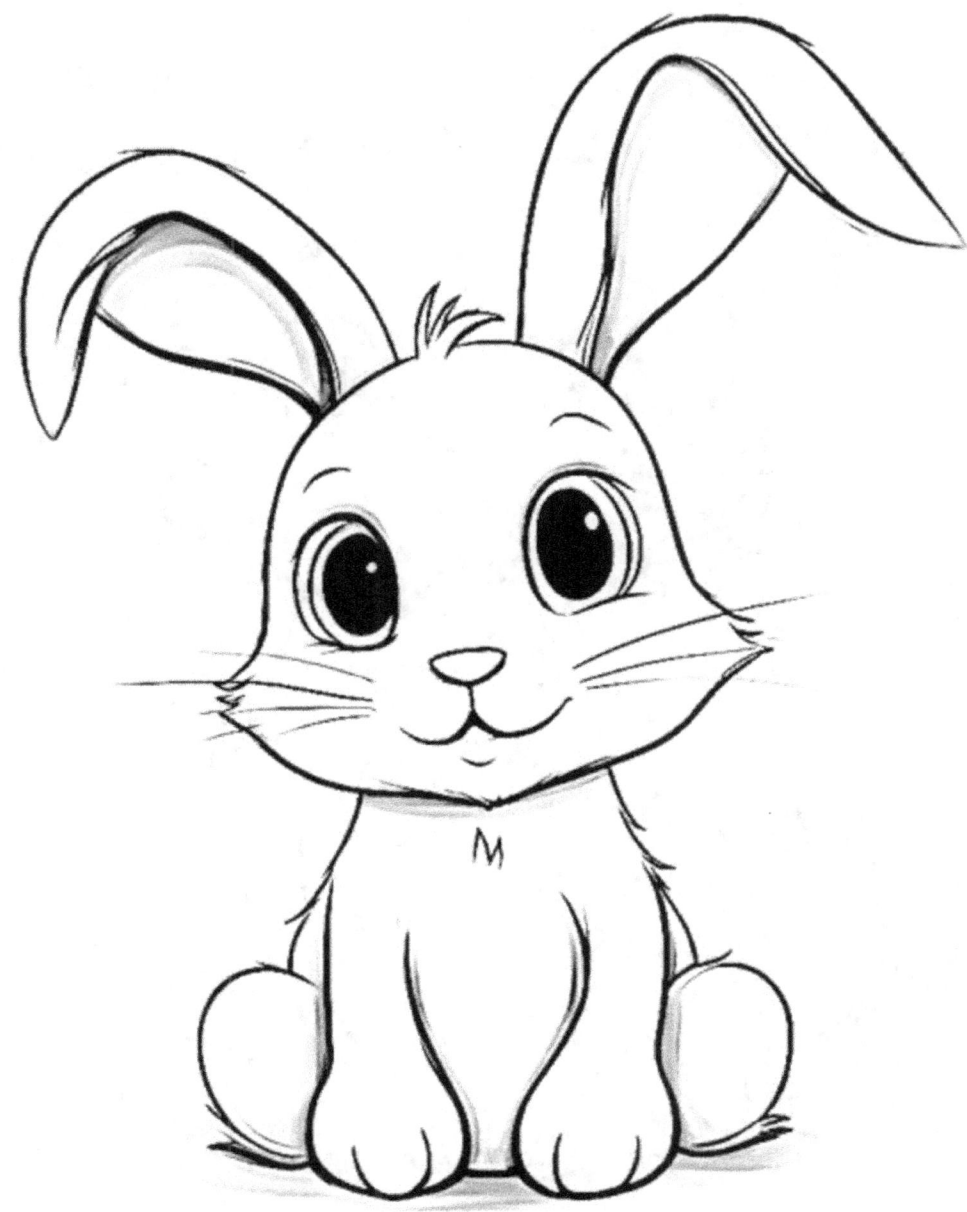

RABBIT

When scanning the QR code, you will be able to see the colored image and, if applicable, listen to the associated sound.

ANALS

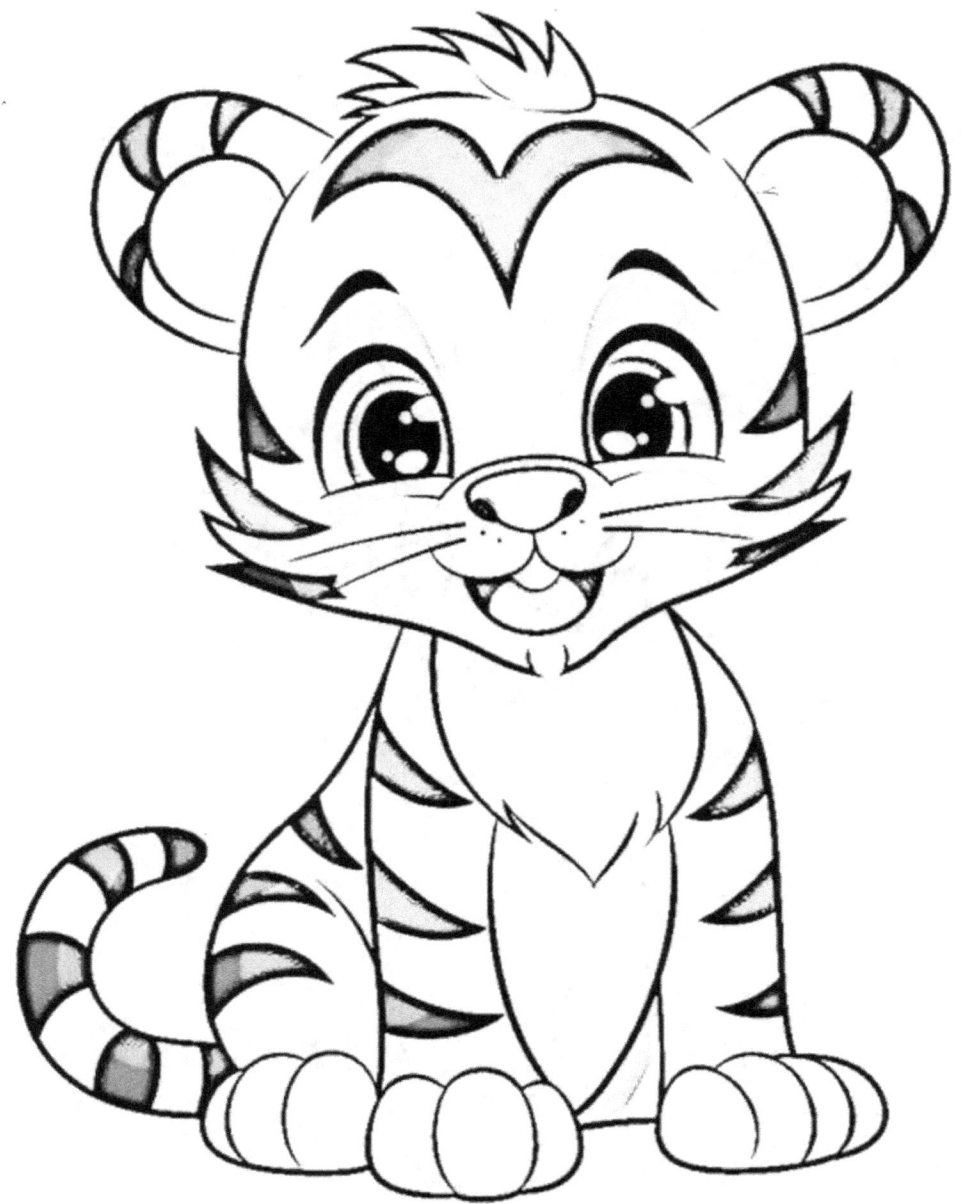

TIGER

When scanning the QR code, you will be able to see the colored image and, if applicable, listen to the associated sound.

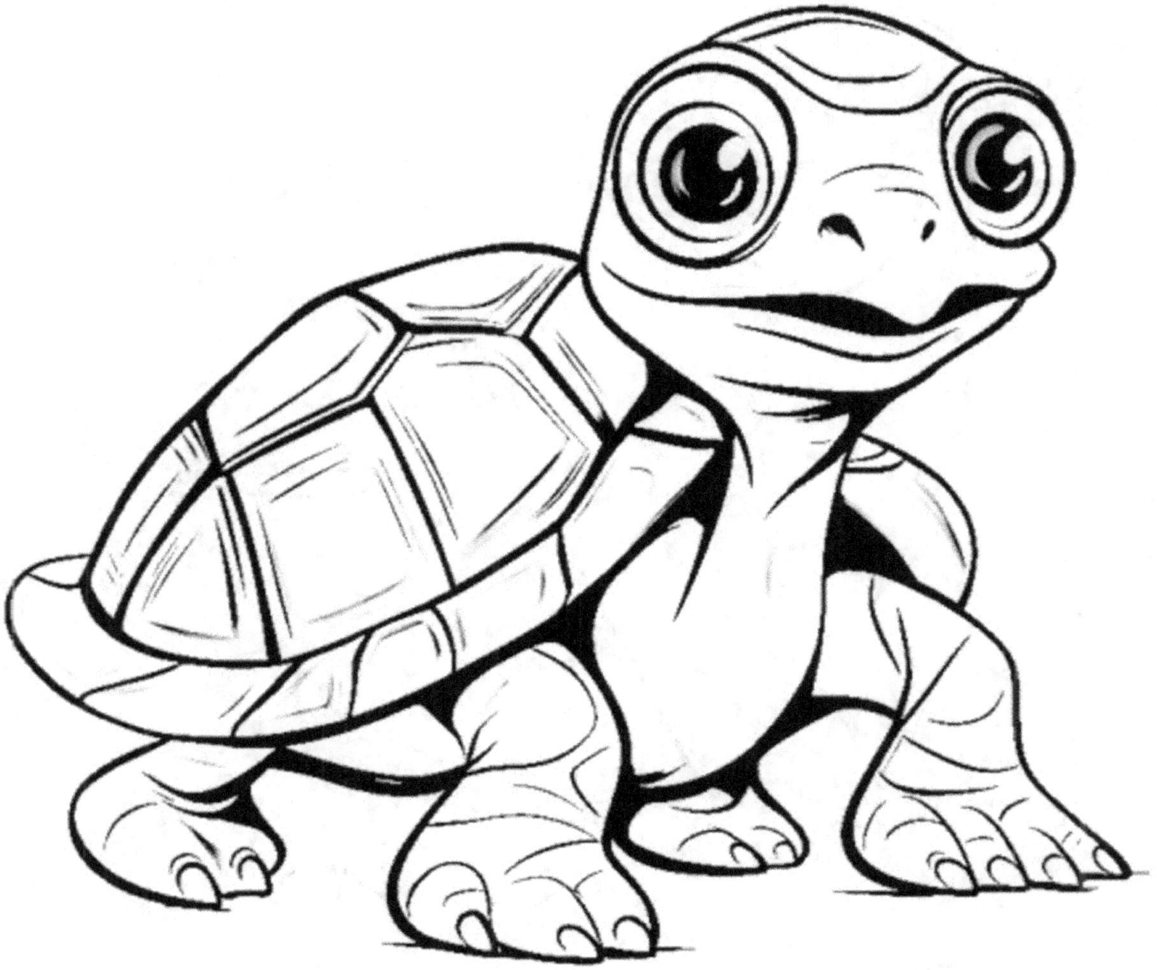

ANIMALS

TORTOISE

When scanning the QR code, you will be able to see the colored image and, if applicable, listen to the associated sound.

ANIMALS

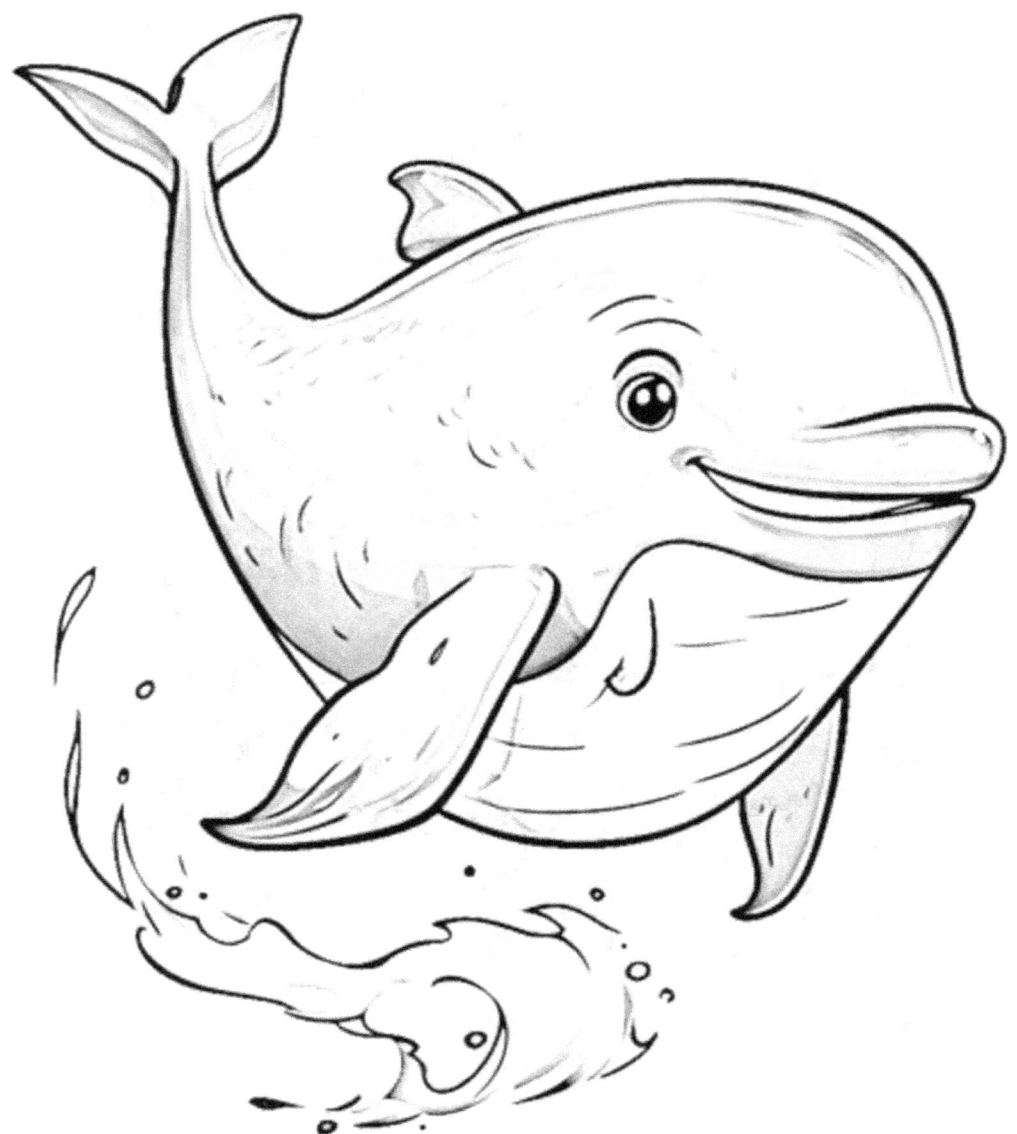

WHALE

When scanning the QR code, you will be able to see the colored image and, if applicable, listen to the associated sound.

ANIMALS

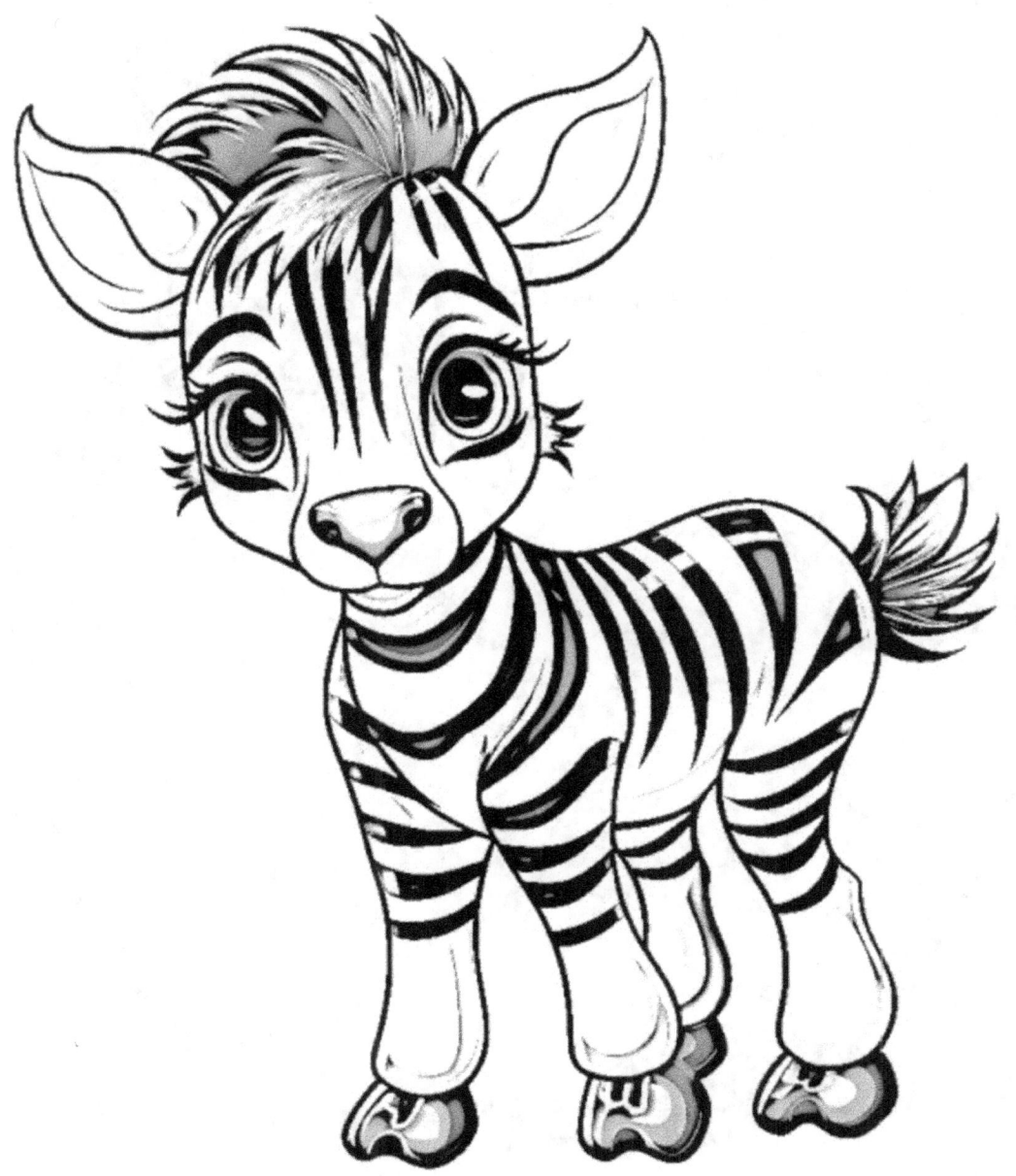

ZEBRA

When scanning the QR code, you will be able to see the colored image and, if applicable, listen to the associated sound.

FRUIT

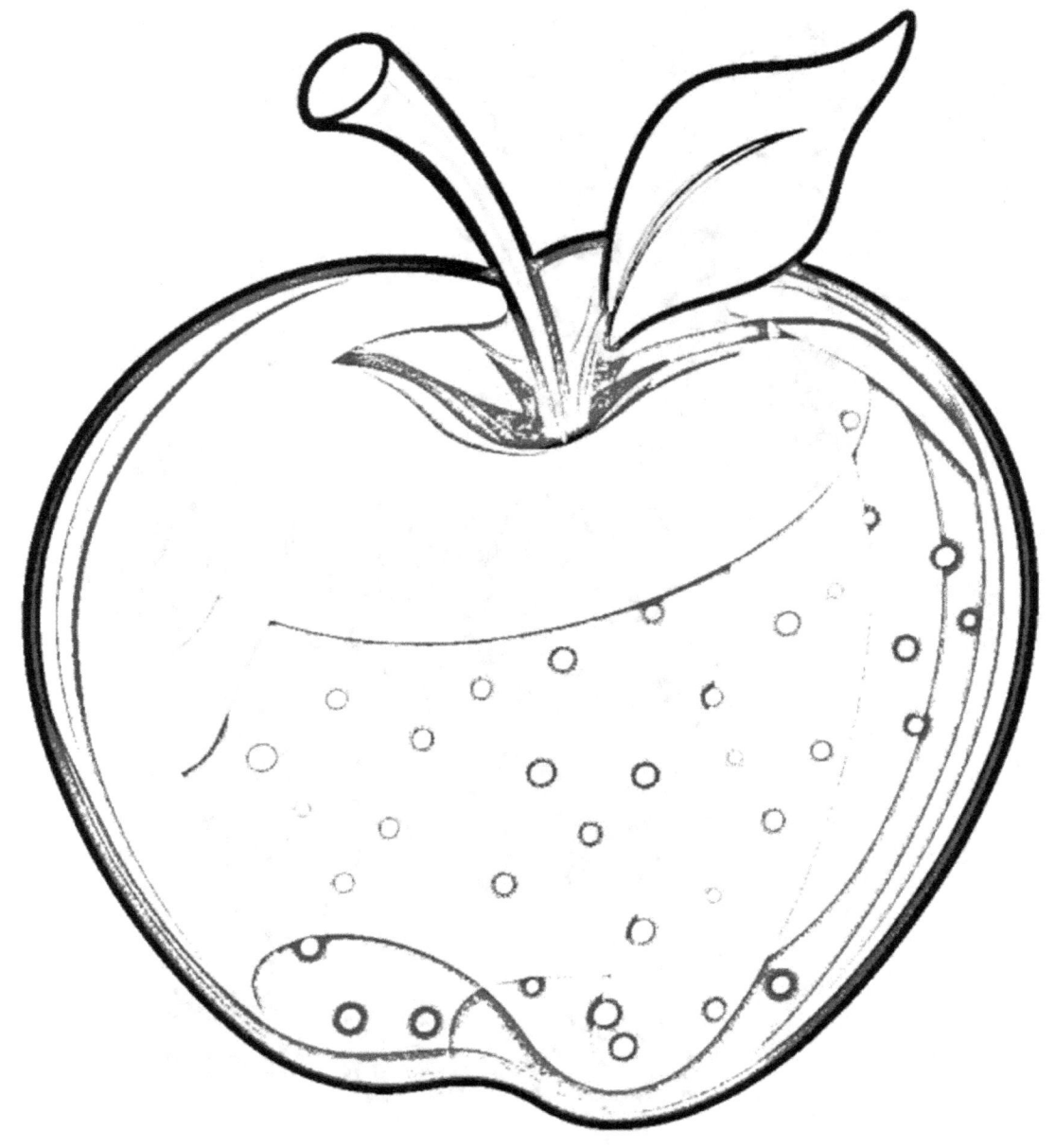

APPLE

When scanning the QR code, you will be able to see the colored image and, if applicable, listen to the associated sound.

FRUIT

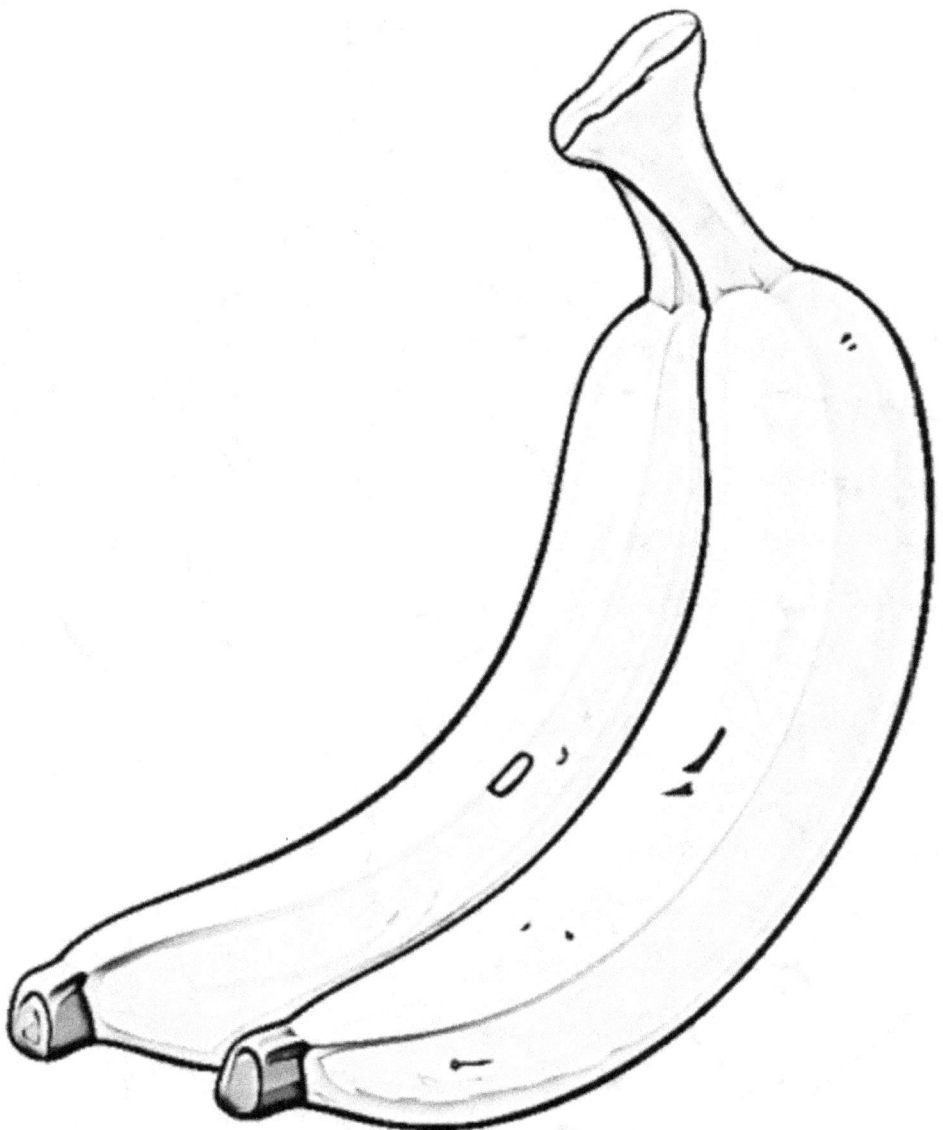

BANANA

When scanning the QR code, you will be able to see the colored image and, if applicable, listen to the associated sound.

FRUIT

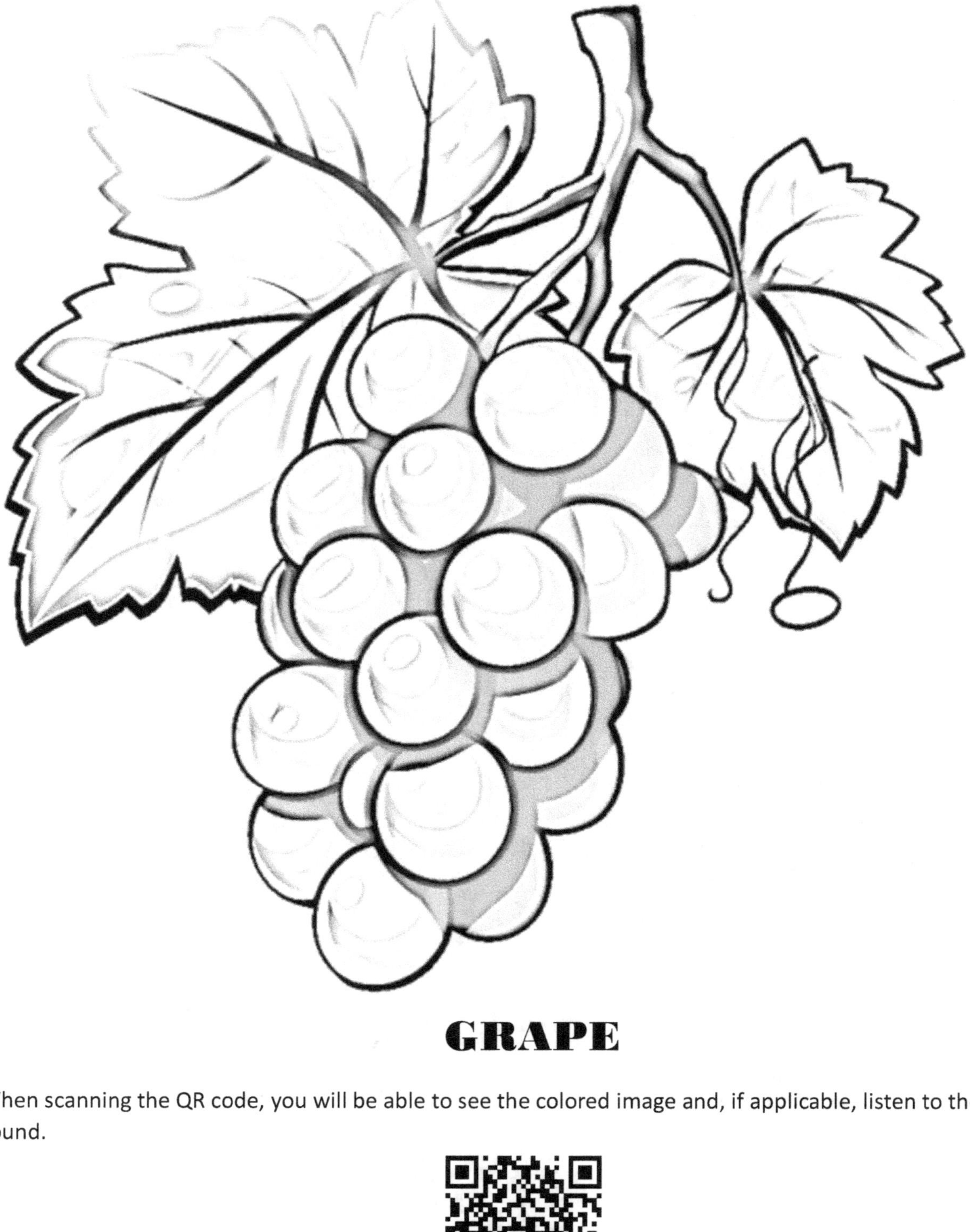

GRAPE

When scanning the QR code, you will be able to see the colored image and, if applicable, listen to the associated sound.

FRUIT

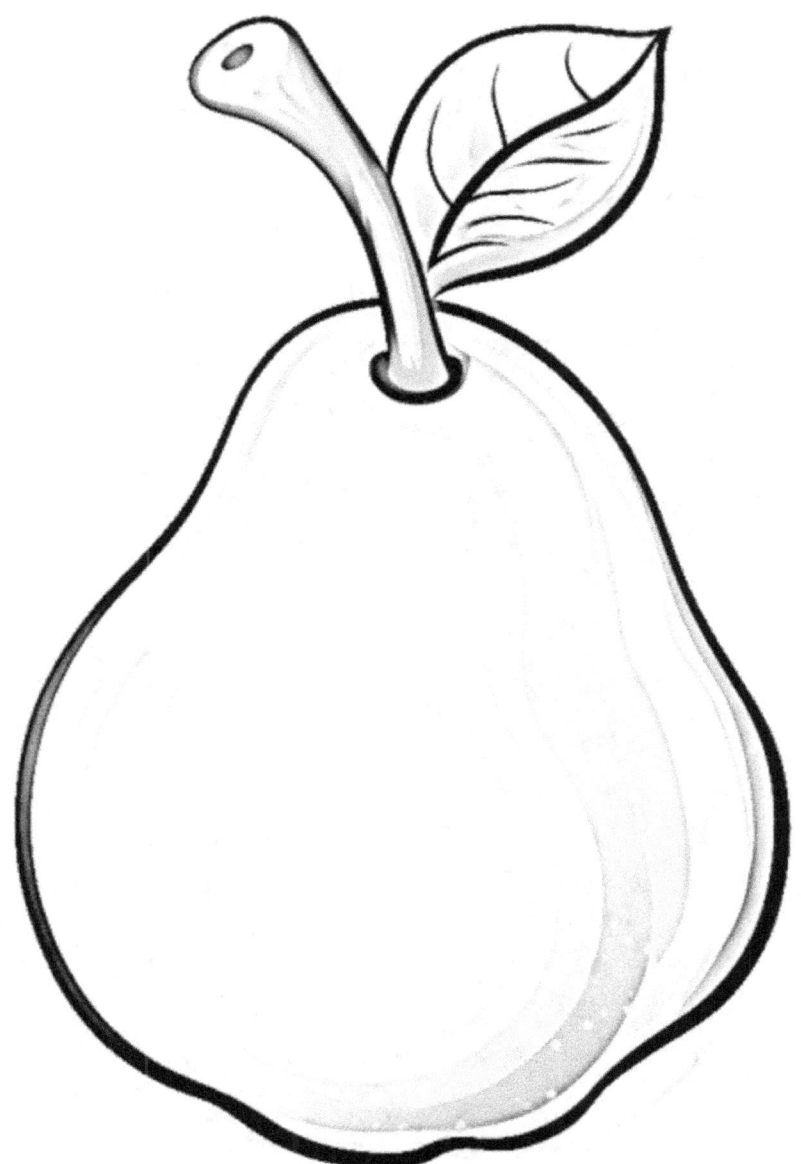

PEAR

When scanning the QR code, you will be able to see the colored image and, if applicable, listen to the associated sound.

FRUIT

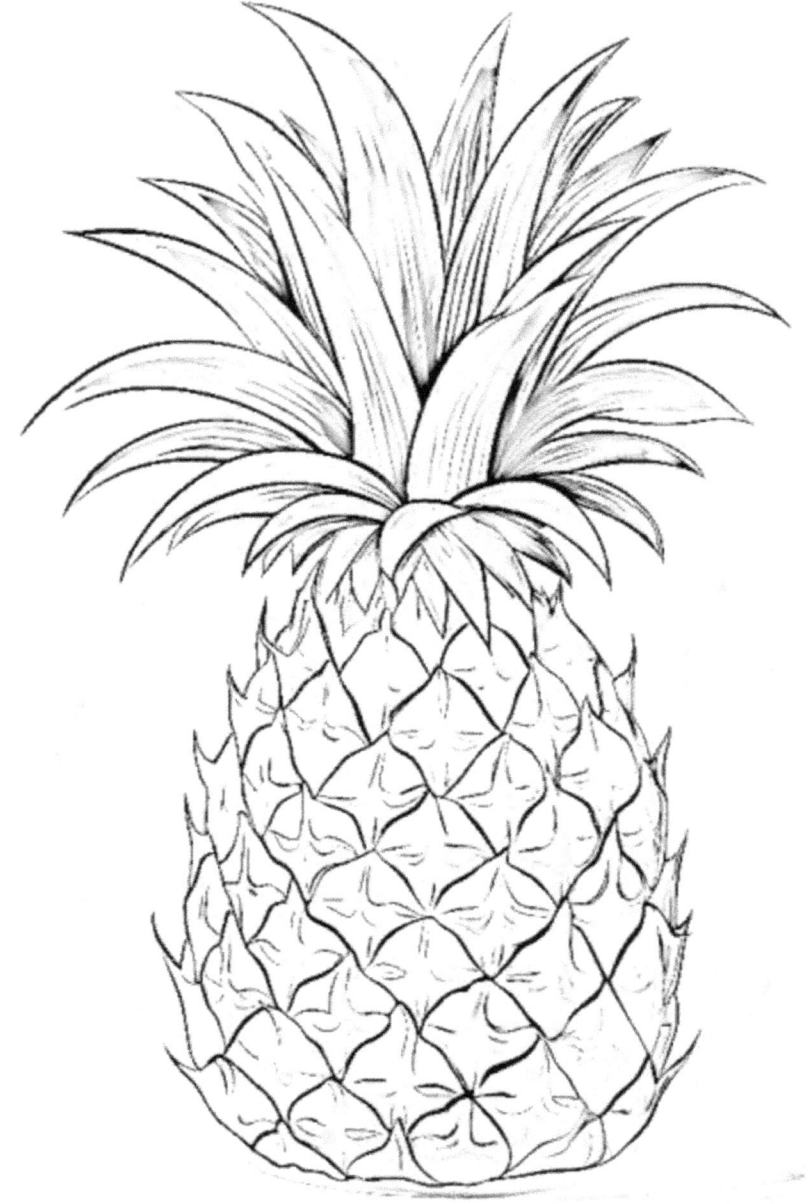

PINEAPPLE

When scanning the QR code, you will be able to see the colored image and, if applicable, listen to the associated sound.

FRUIT

STRAWBERRY

When scanning the QR code, you will be able to see the colored image and, if applicable, listen to the associated sound.

FRUIT

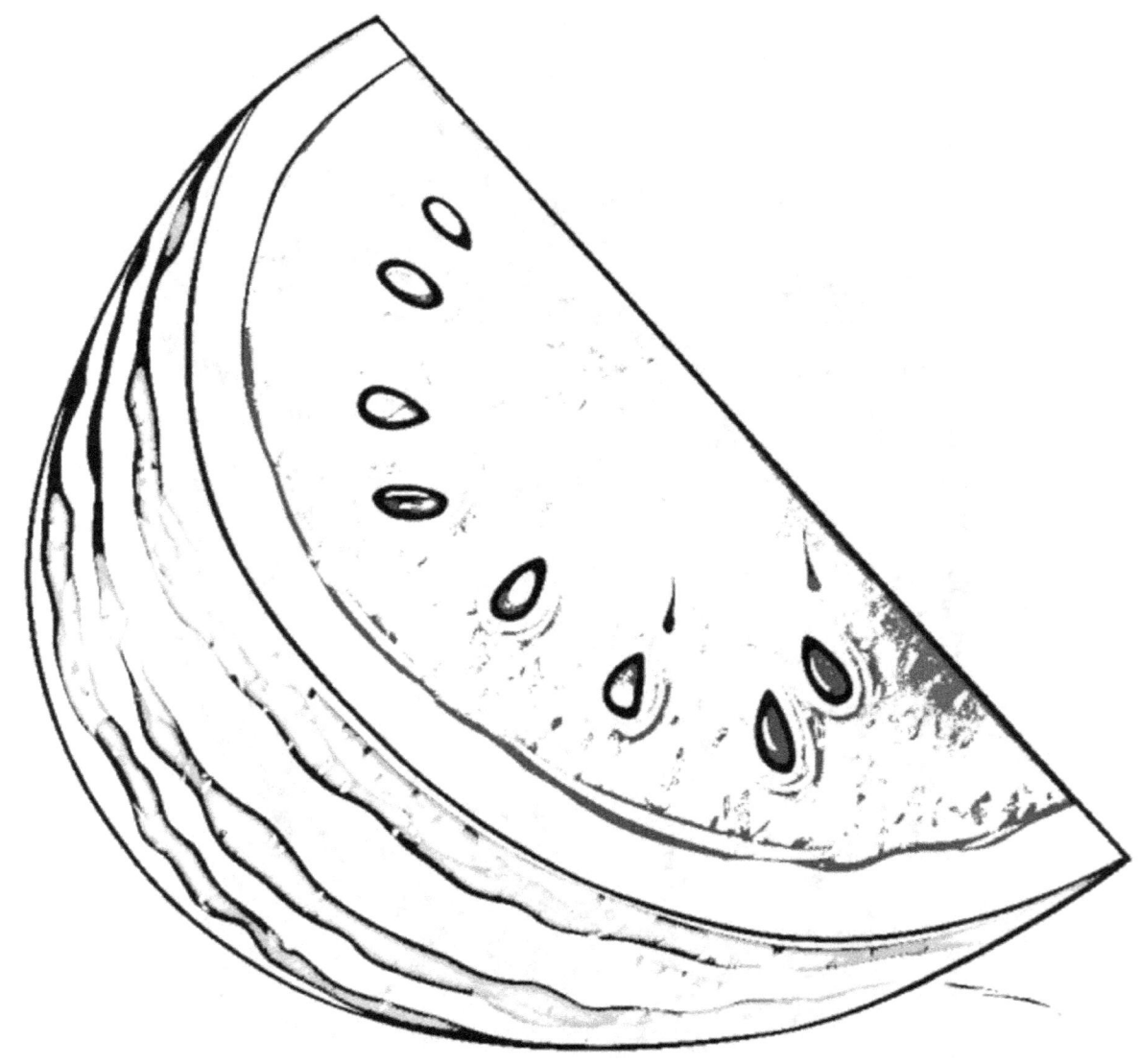

WATERMELON

When scanning the QR code, you will be able to see the colored image and, if applicable, listen to the associated sound.

PEOPLE

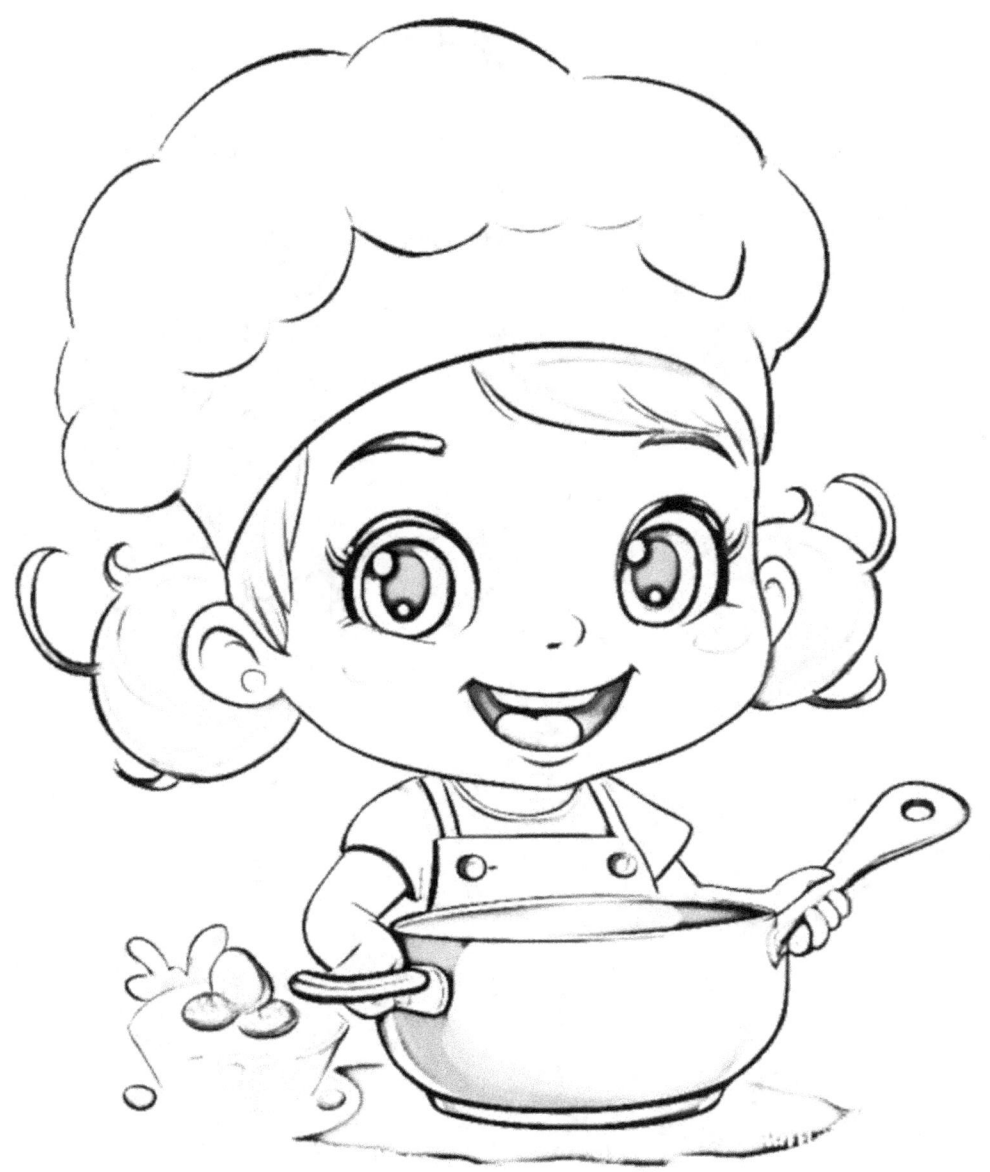

CHEF

When scanning the QR code, you will be able to see the colored image and, if applicable, listen to the associated sound.

PEOPLE

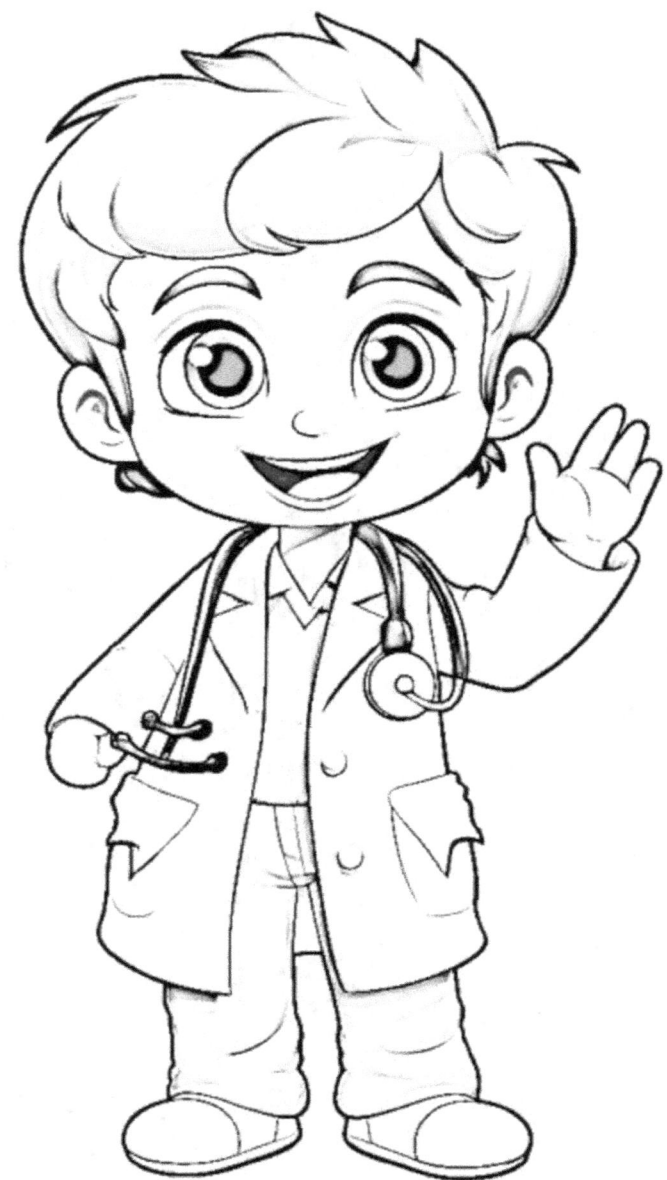

DOCTOR

When scanning the QR code, you will be able to see the colored image and, if applicable, listen to the associated sound.

PEOPLE

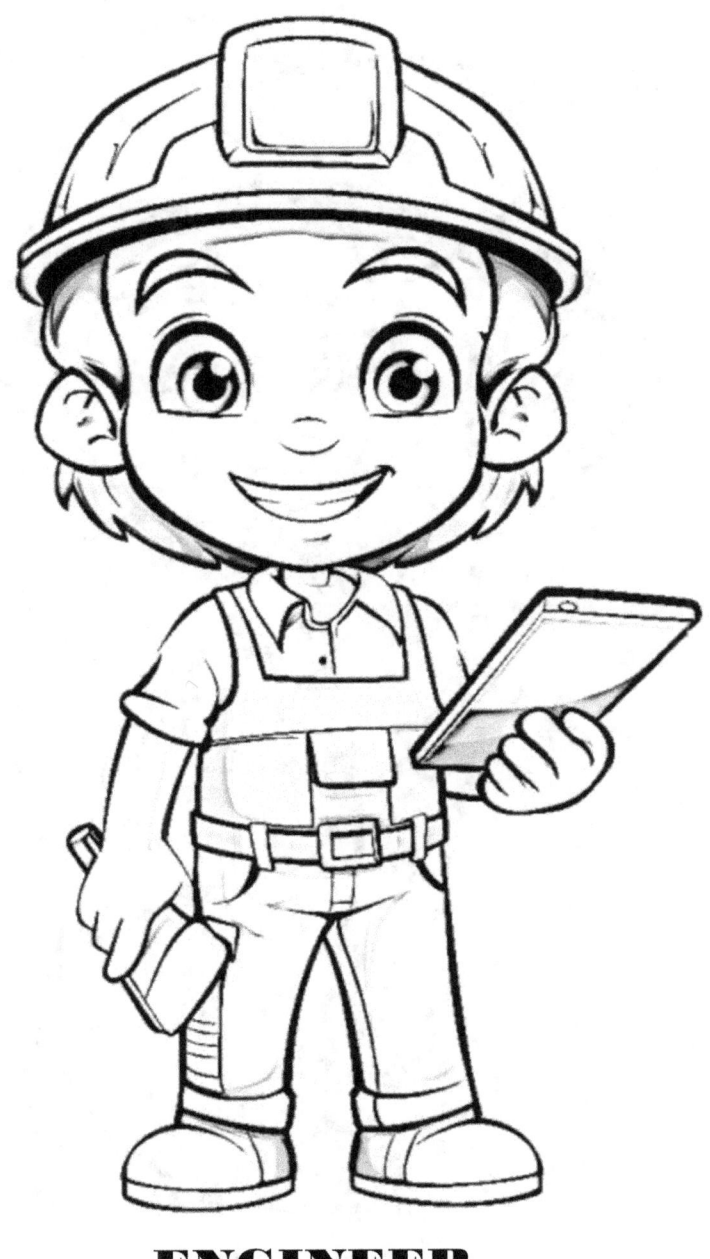

ENGINEER

When scanning the QR code, you will be able to see the colored image and, if applicable, listen to the associated sound.

PEOPLE

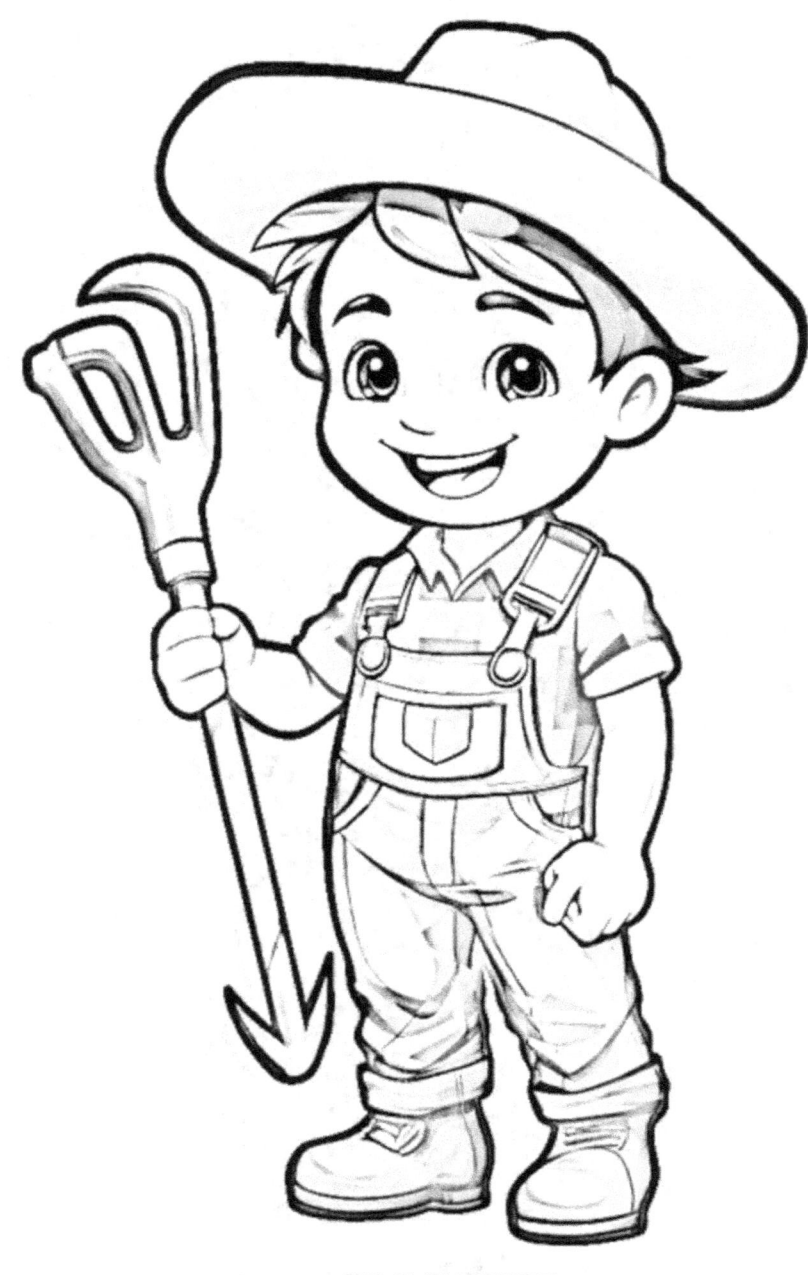

FAMER

When scanning the QR code, you will be able to see the colored image and, if applicable, listen to the associated sound.

PEOPLE

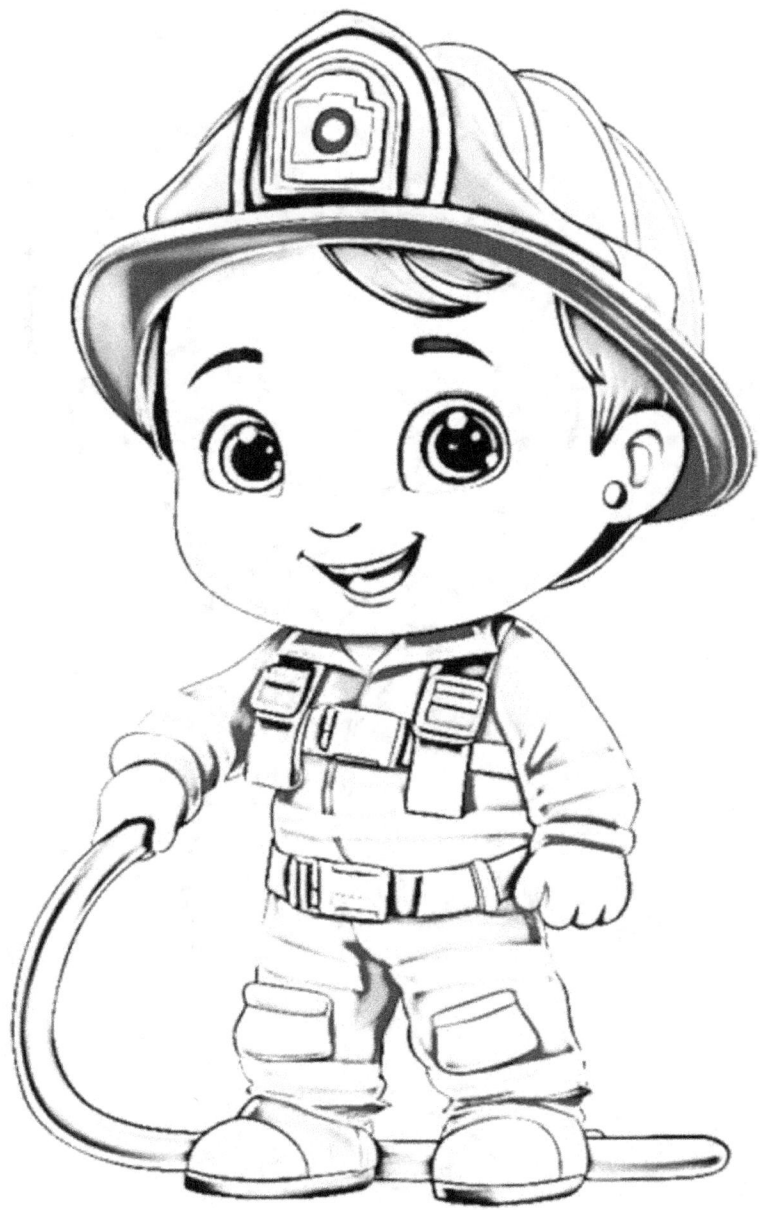

FIREMAN

When scanning the QR code, you will be able to see the colored image and, if applicable, listen to the associated sound.

PEOPLE

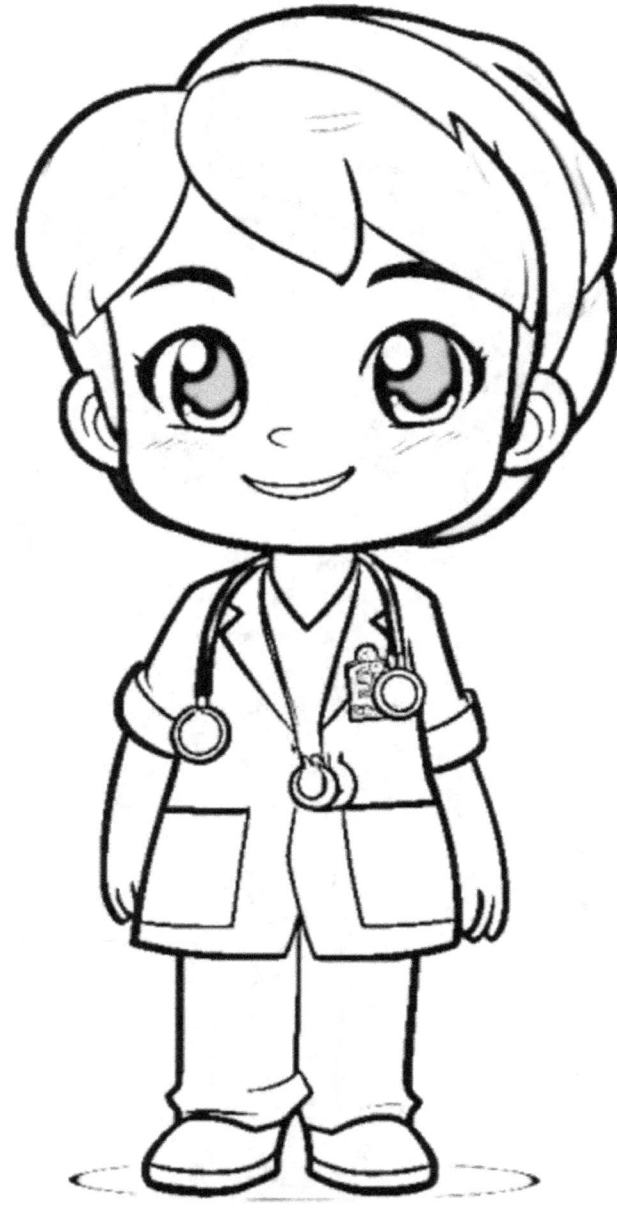

NURSE

When scanning the QR code, you will be able to see the colored image and, if applicable, listen to the associated sound.

PEOPLE

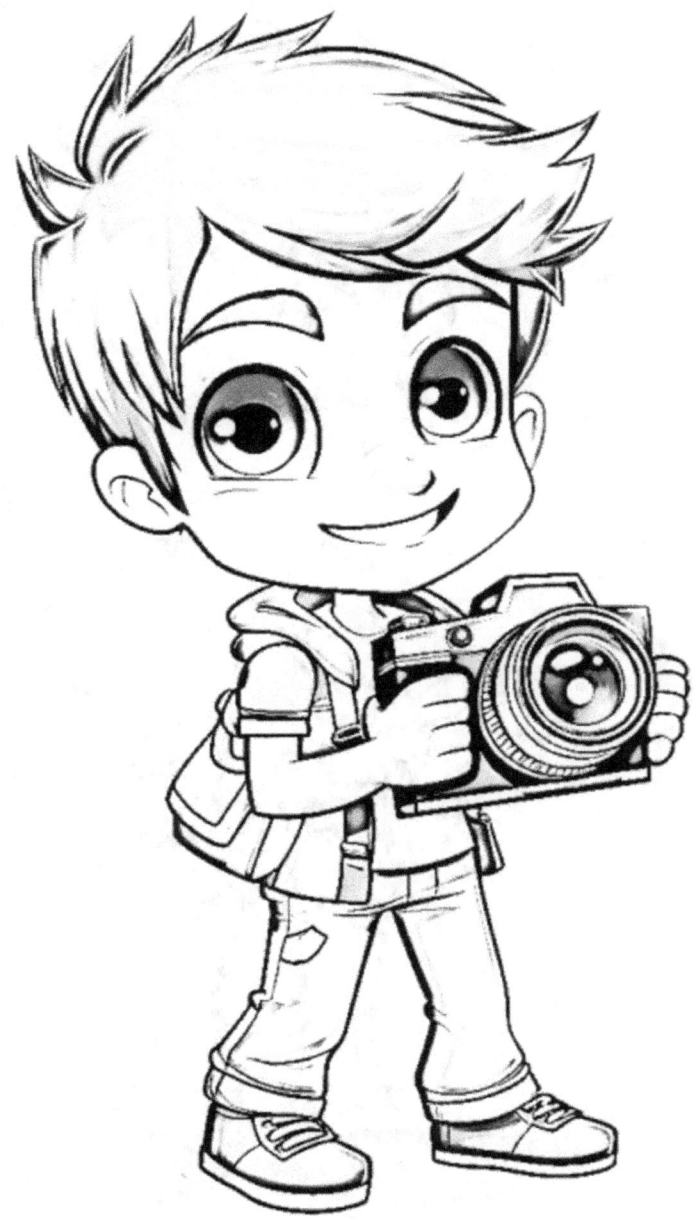

PHOTOGRAPHER

When scanning the QR code, you will be able to see the colored image and, if applicable, listen to the associated sound.

PEOPLE

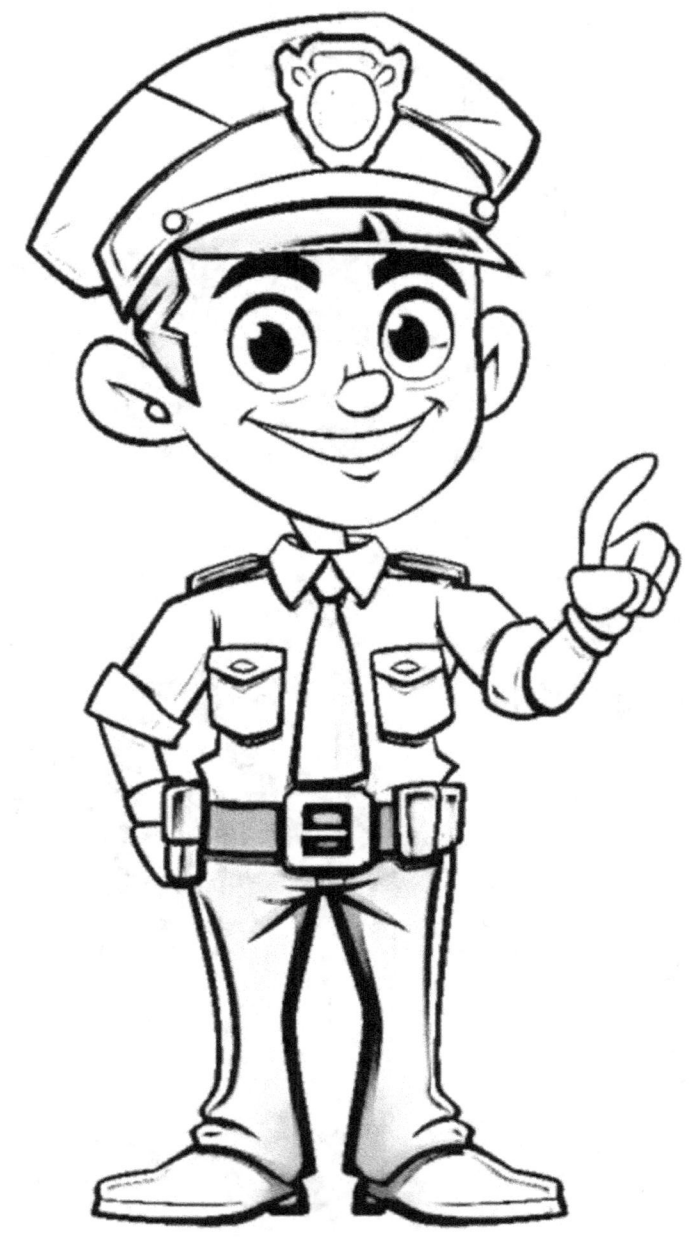

POLICE

When scanning the QR code, you will be able to see the colored image and, if applicable, listen to the associated sound.

PEOPLE

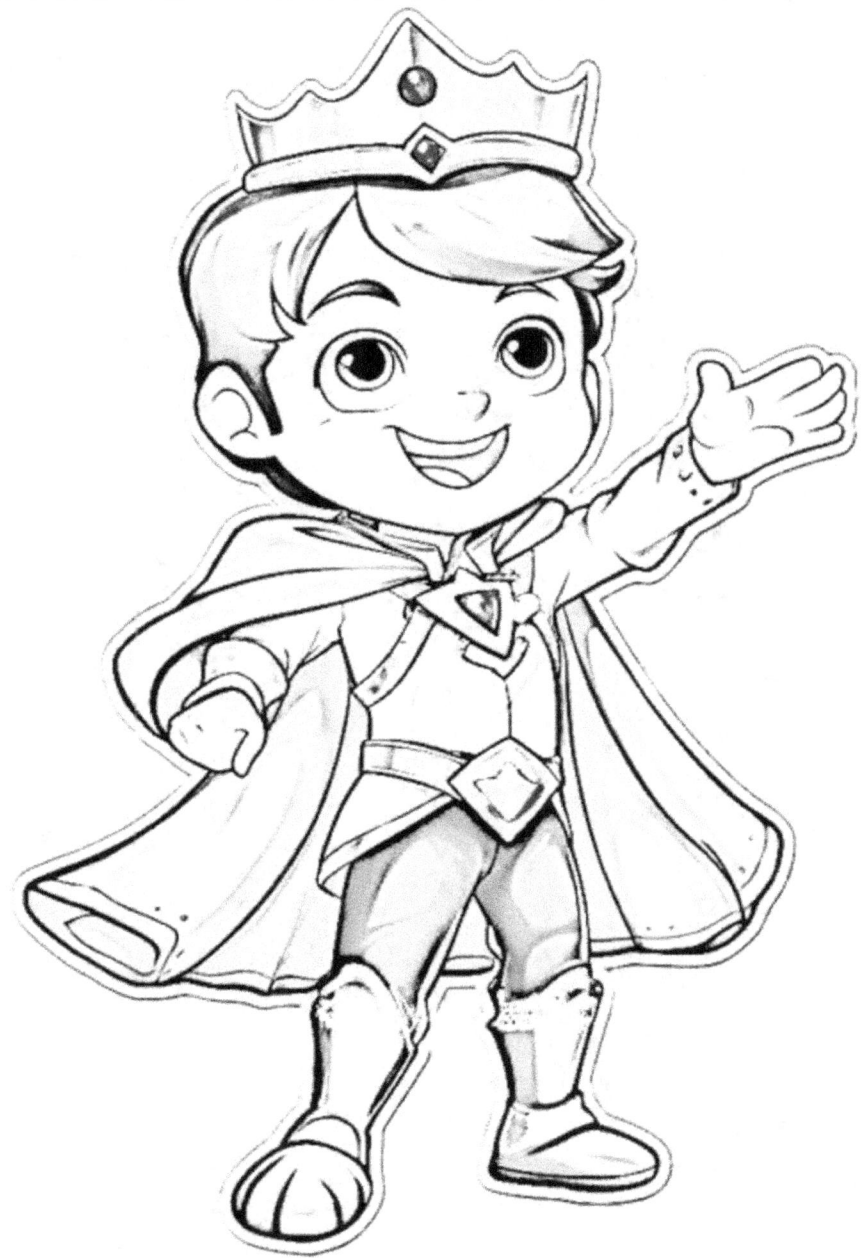

PRINCE

When scanning the QR code, you will be able to see the colored image and, if applicable, listen to the associated sound.

PEOPLE

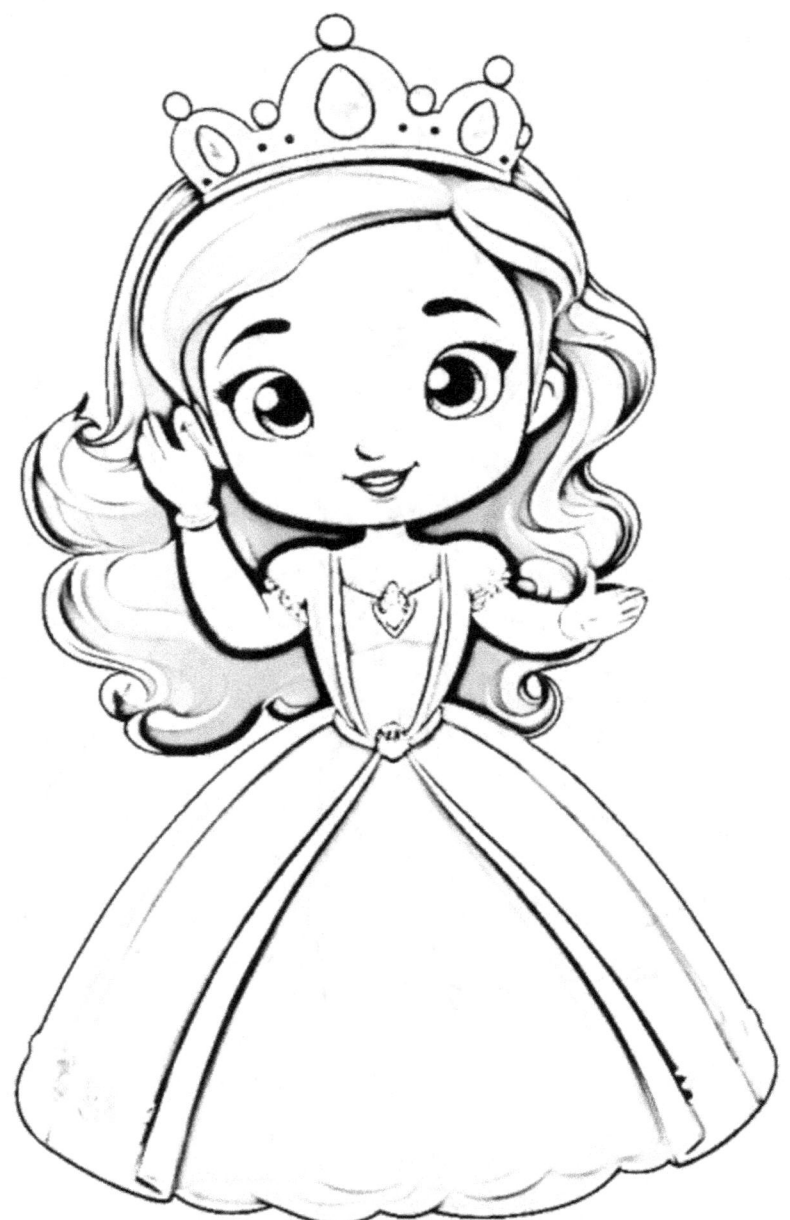

PRINCESS

When scanning the QR code, you will be able to see the colored image and, if applicable, listen to the associated sound.

PEOPLE

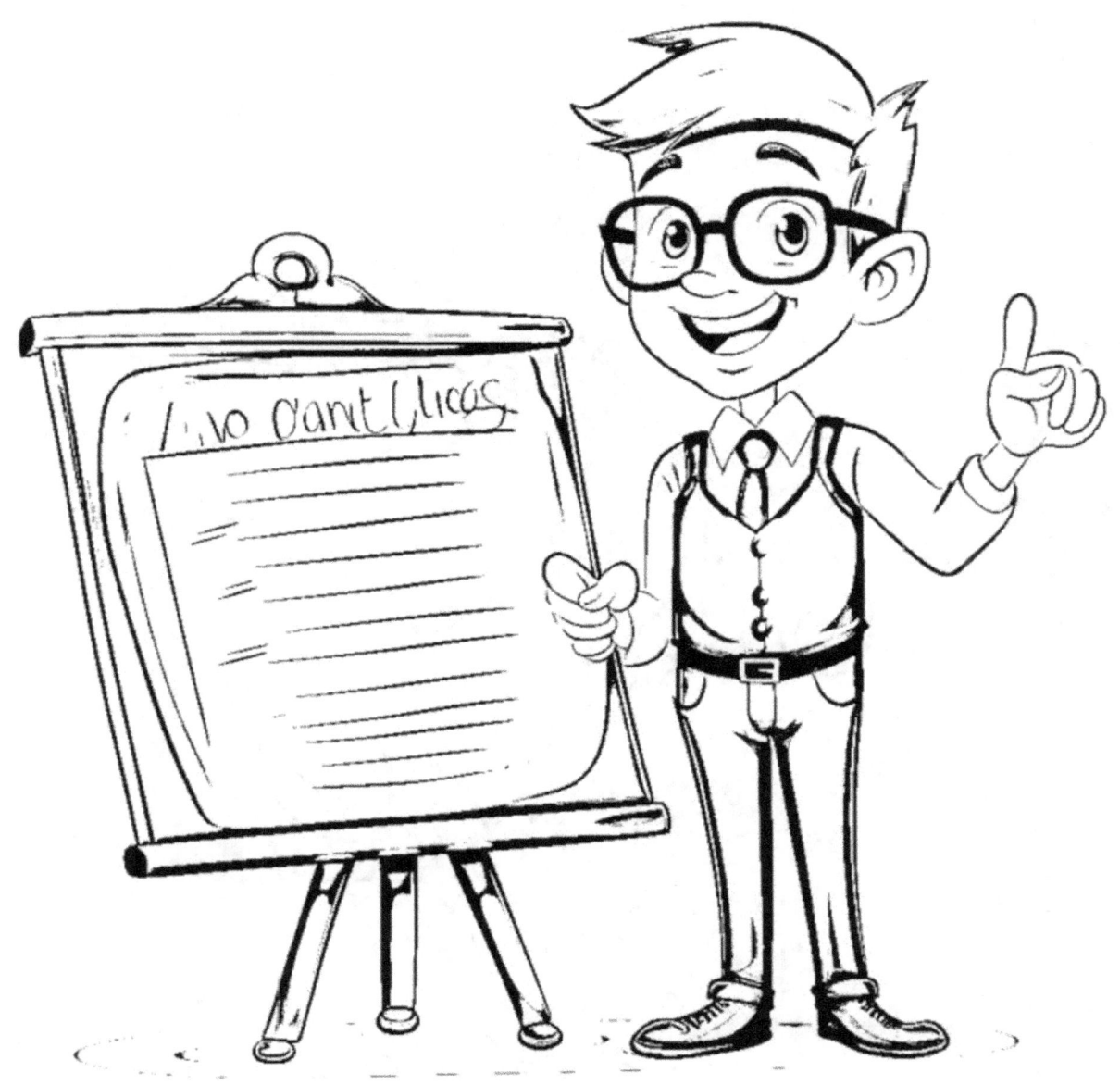

TEACHE

When scanning the QR code, you will be able to see the colored image and, if applicable, listen to the associated sound.

FLOWERS

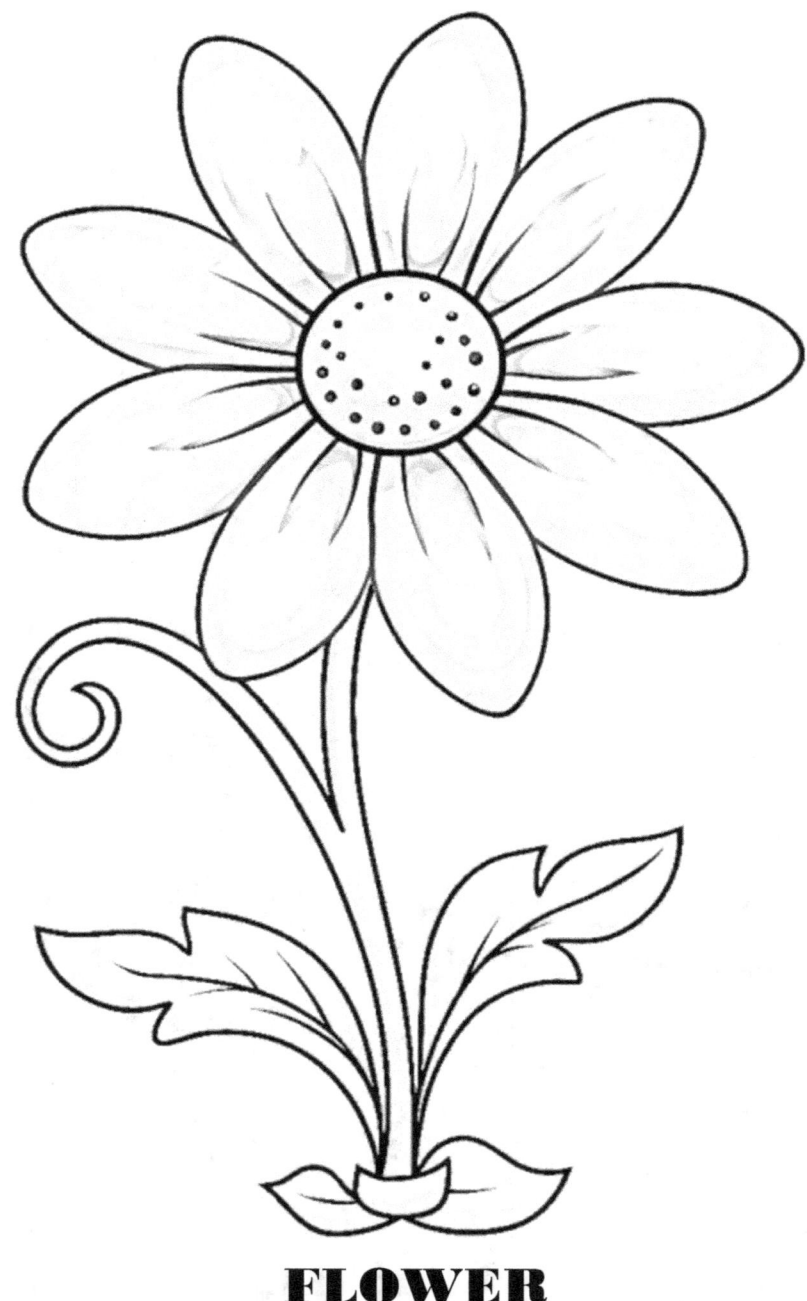

FLOWER

When scanning the QR code, you will be able to see the colored image and, if applicable, listen to the associated sound.

FLOWERS

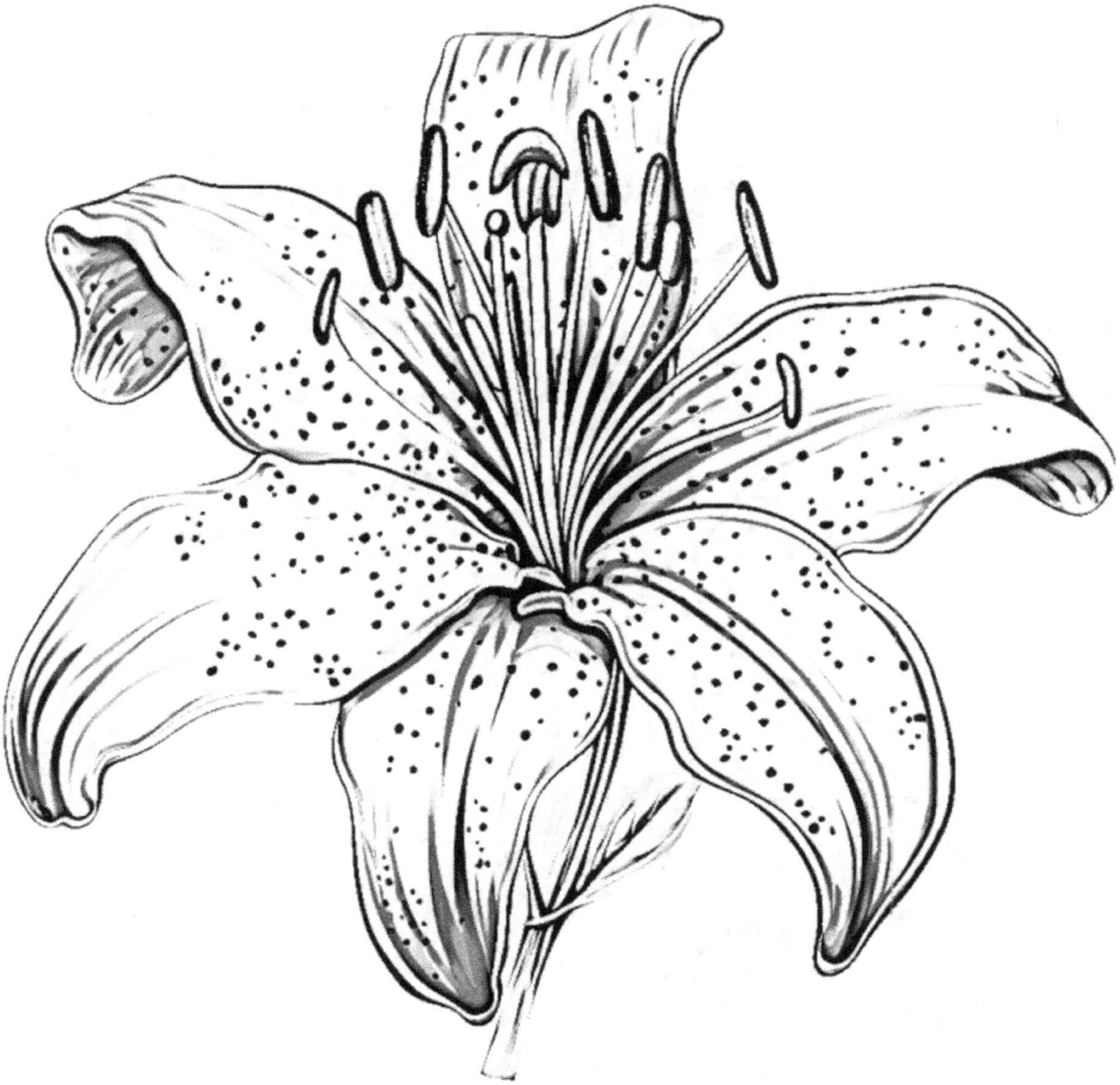

LILY

When scanning the QR code, you will be able to see the colored image and, if applicable, listen to the associated sound.

FLOWERS

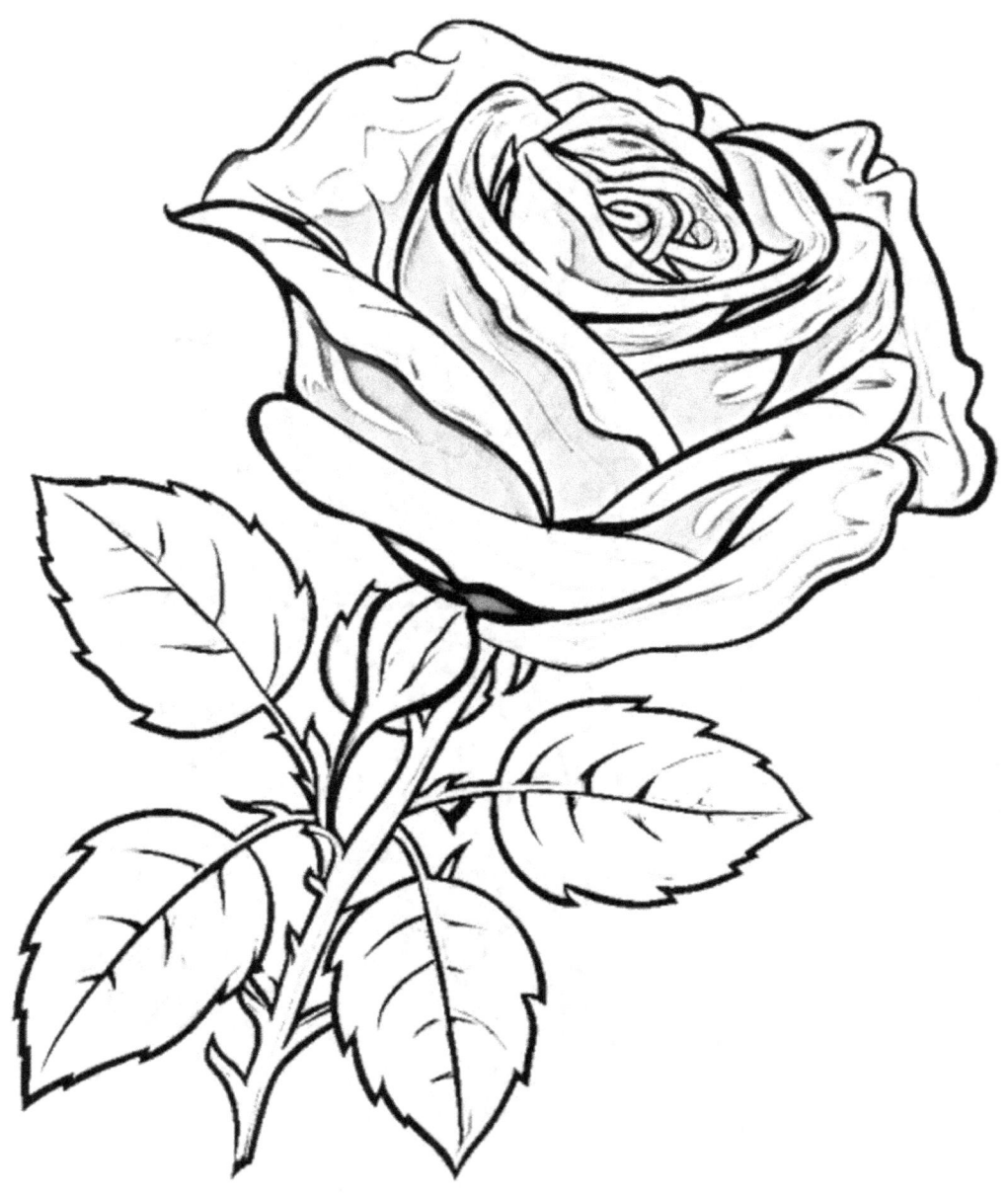

ROSE

When scanning the QR code, you will be able to see the colored image and, if applicable, listen to the associated sound.

FLOWERS

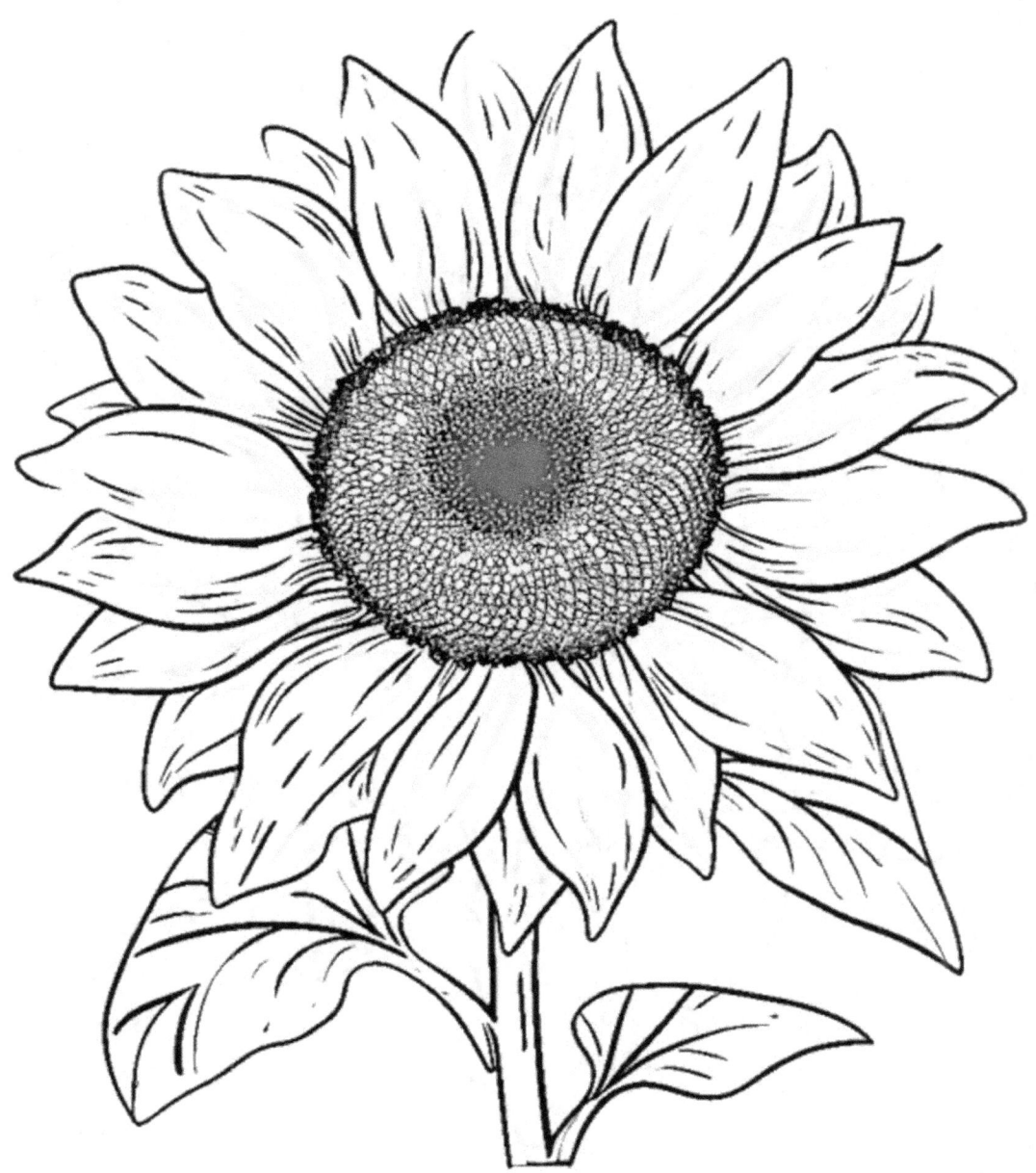

SUNFLOWER

When scanning the QR code, you will be able to see the colored image and, if applicable, listen to the associated sound.

FLOWERS

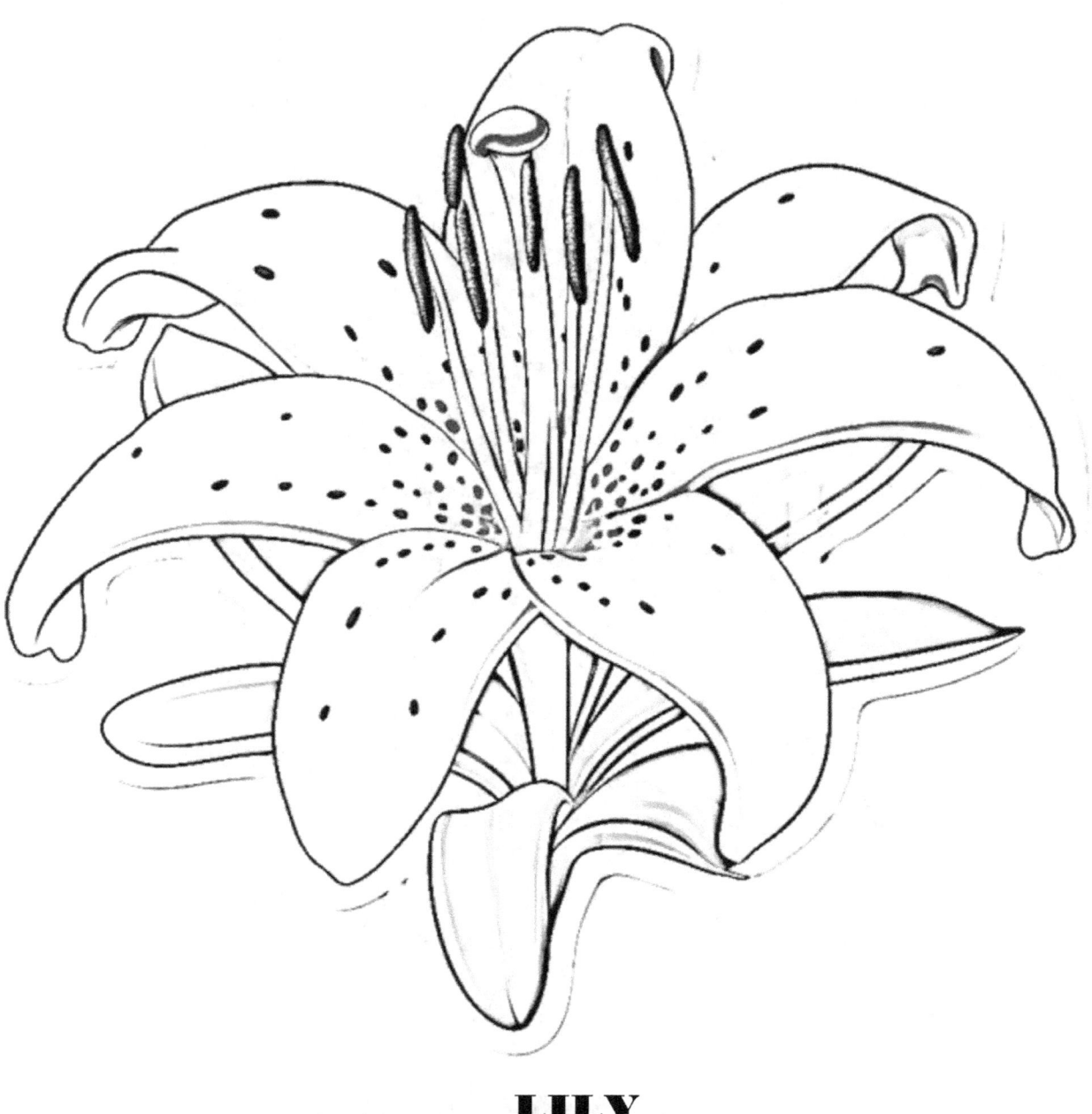

LILY

When scanning the QR code, you will be able to see the colored image and, if applicable, listen to the associated sound.

FLOWERS

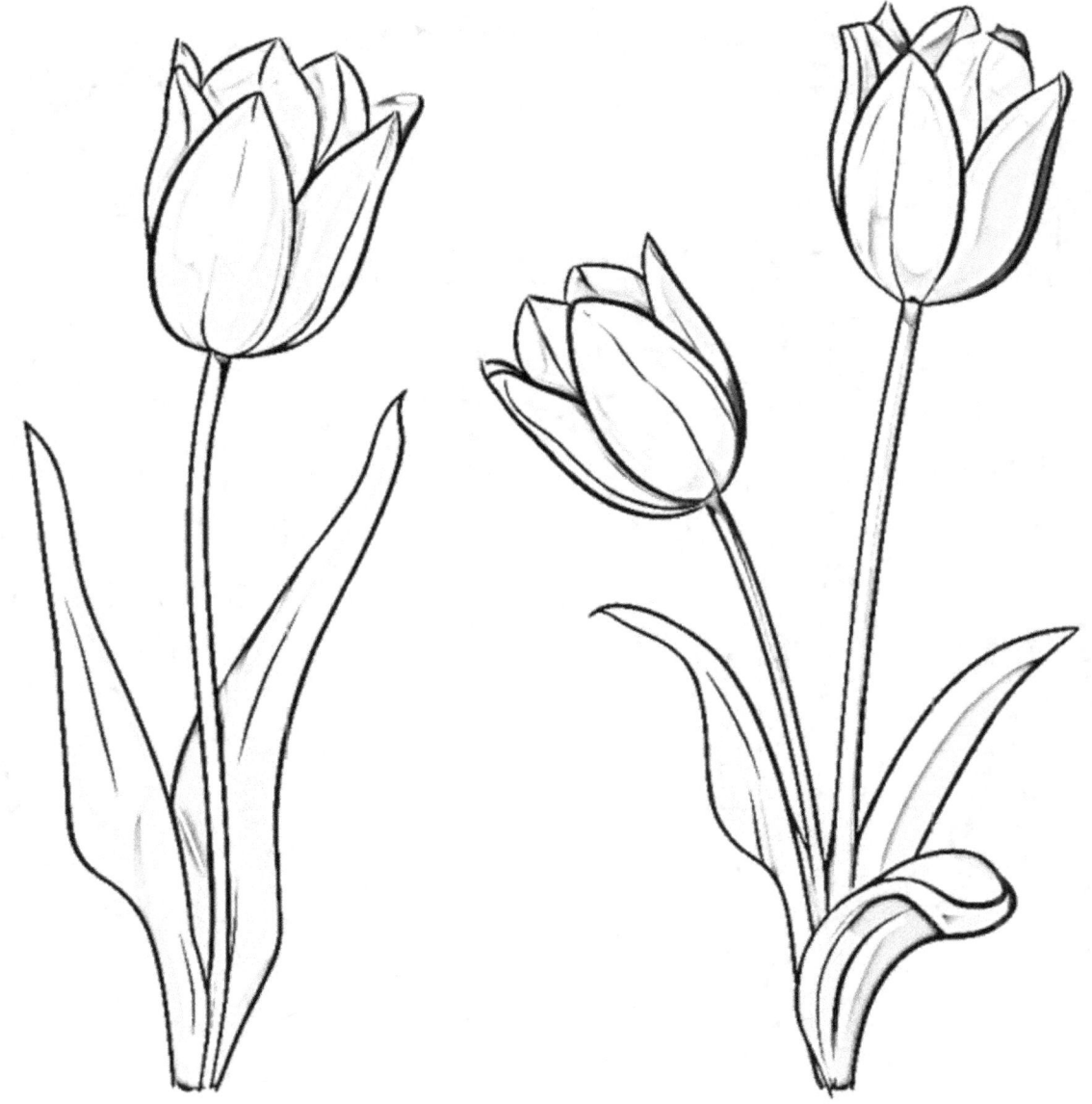

TULIP

When scanning the QR code, you will be able to see the colored image and, if applicable, listen to the associated sound.

MUSICAL INSTRUMENTS

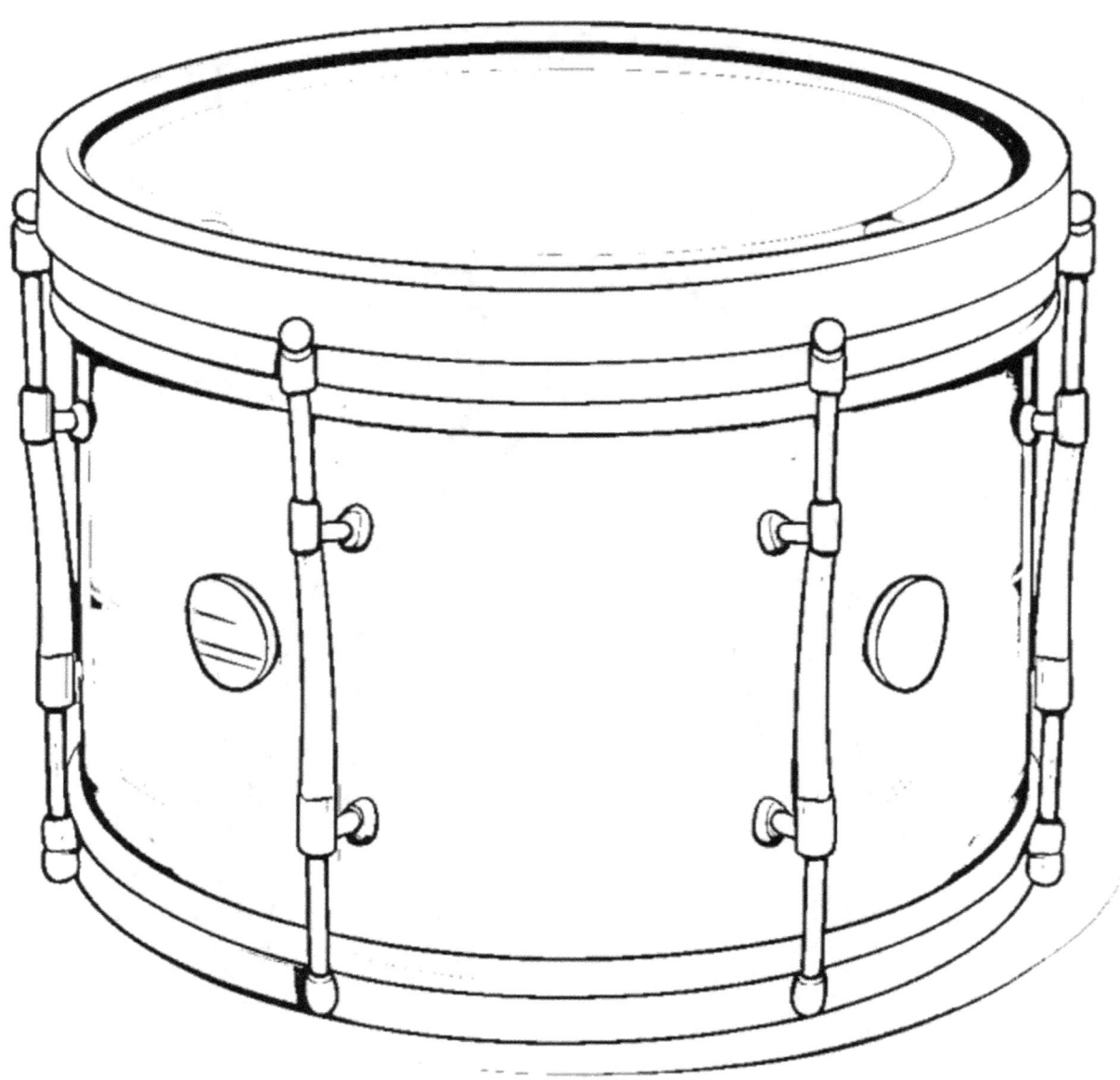

DRUM

When scanning the QR code, you will be able to see the colored image and, if applicable, listen to the associated sound.

MUSICAL INSTRUMENTS

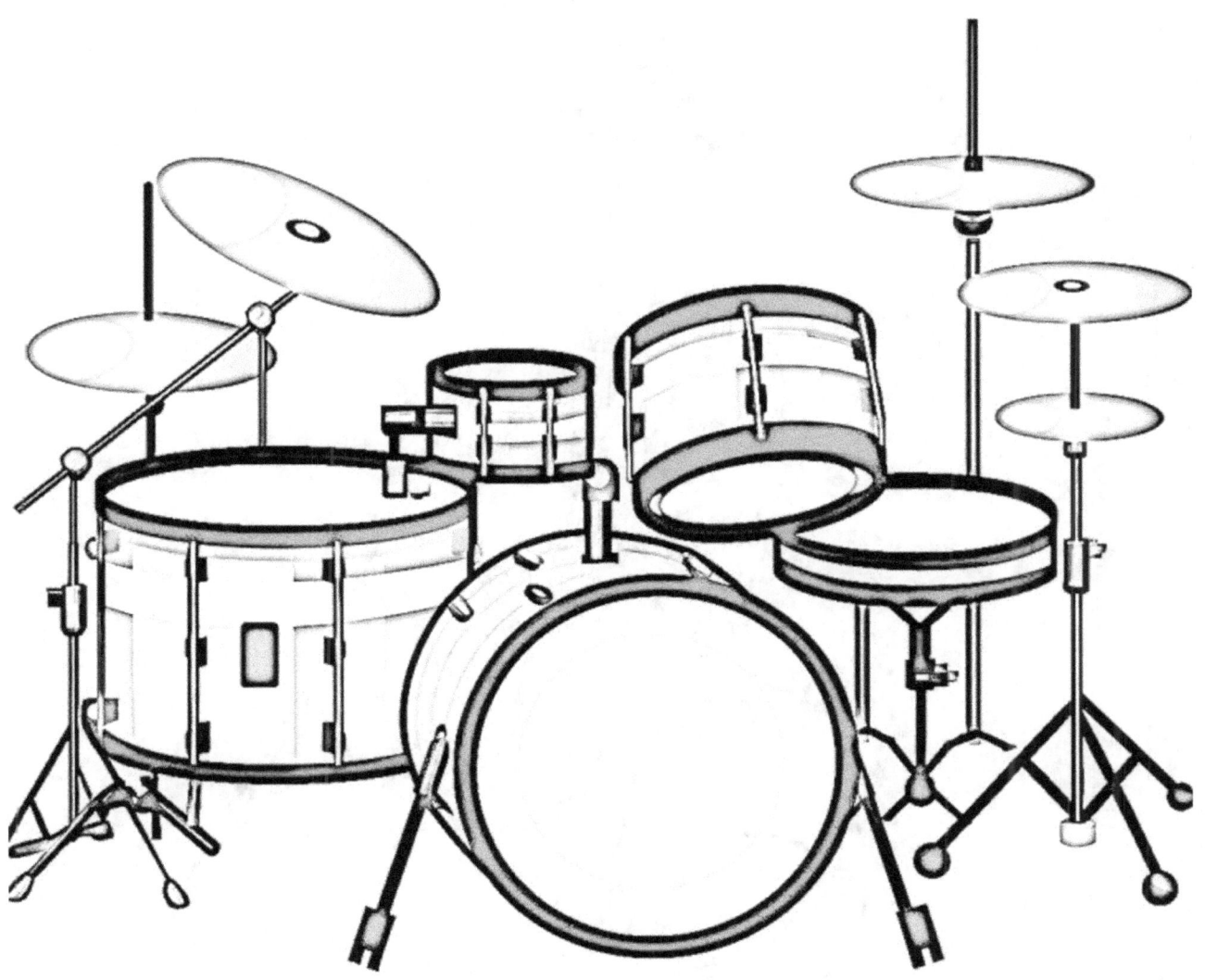

DRUMS

When scanning the QR code, you will be able to see the colored image and, if applicable, listen to the associated sound.

MUSICAL INSTRUMENTS

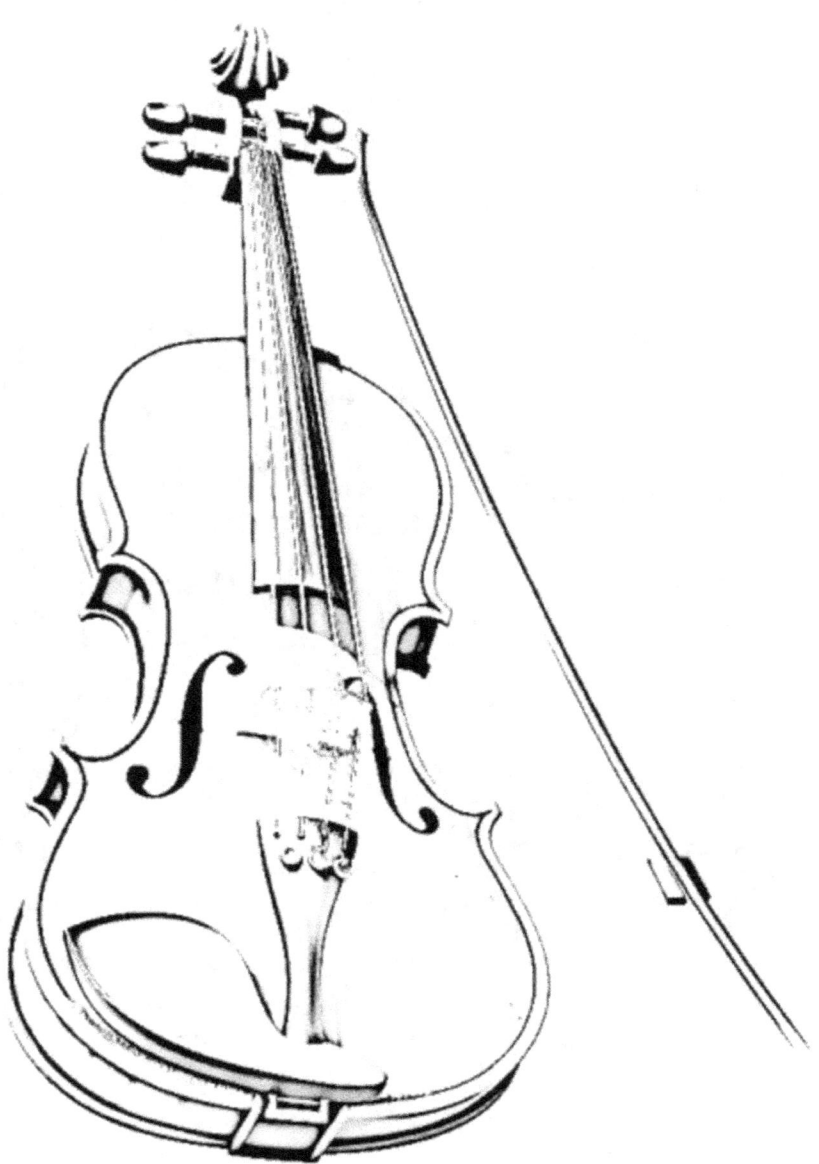

FIDDLE

When scanning the QR code, you will be able to see the colored image and, if applicable, listen to the associated sound.

MUSICAL INSTRUMENTS

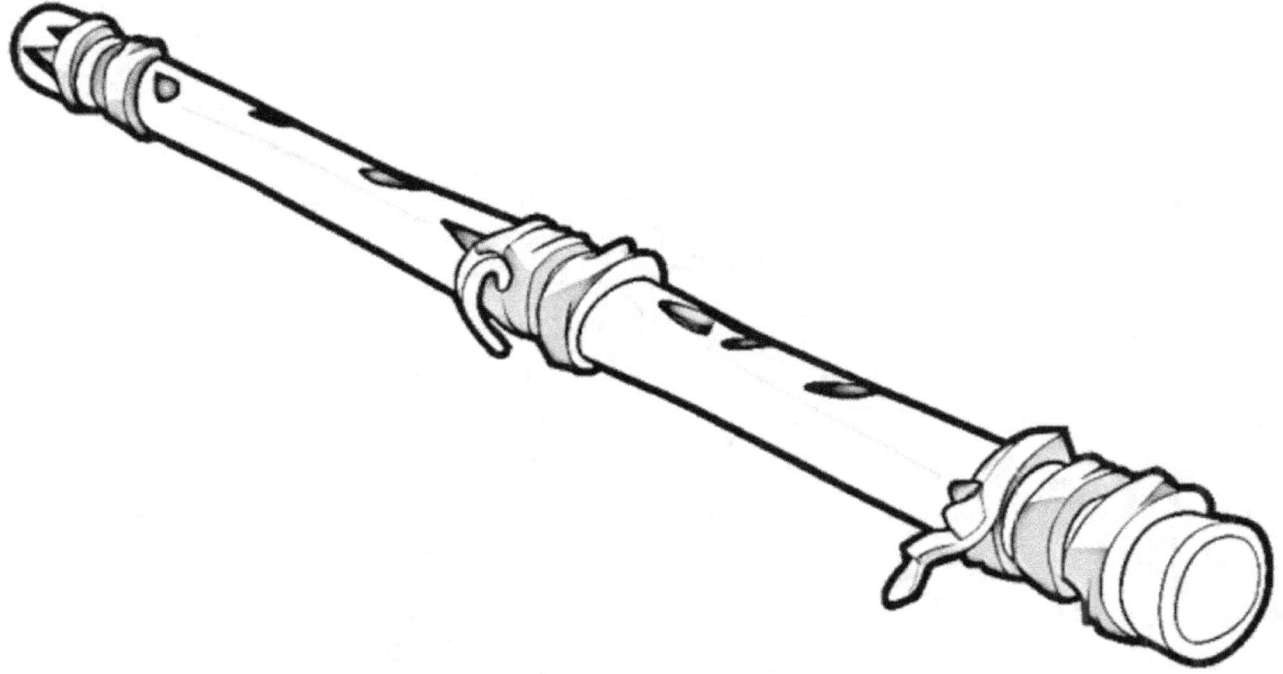

FLUTE

When scanning the QR code, you will be able to see the colored image and, if applicable, listen to the associated sound.

MUSICAL INSTRUMENTS

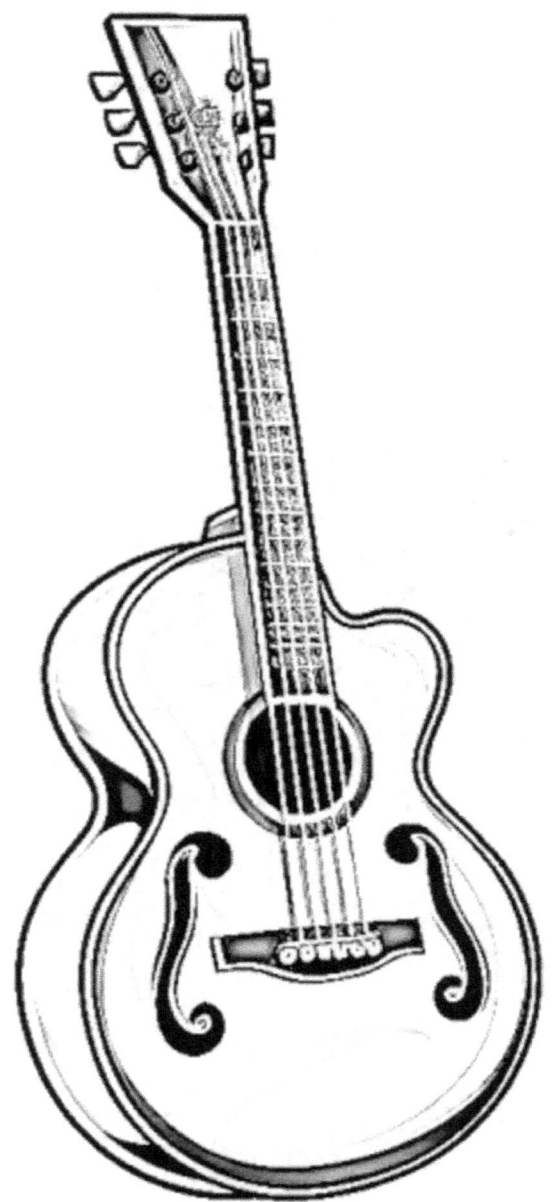

GUITAR

When scanning the QR code, you will be able to see the colored image and, if applicable, listen to the associated sound.

MUSICAL INSTRUMENTS

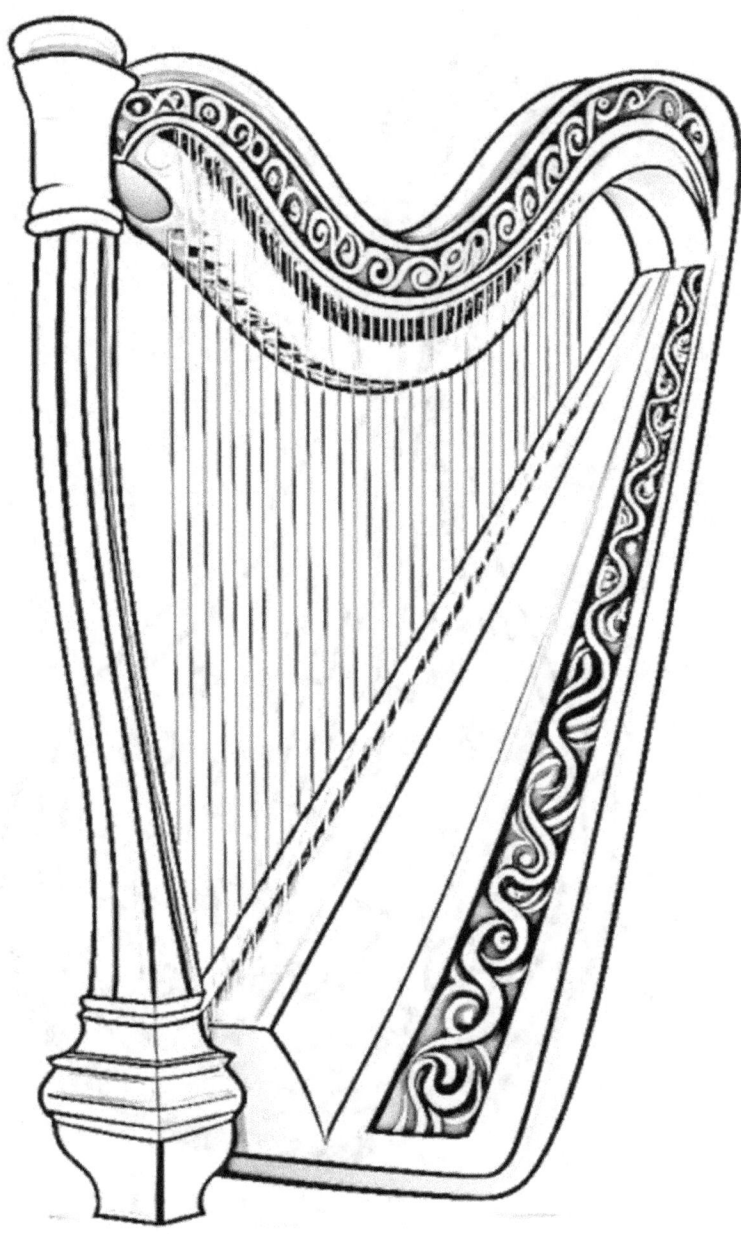

HARP

When scanning the QR code, you will be able to see the colored image and, if applicable, listen to the associated sound.

MUSICAL INSTRUMENTS

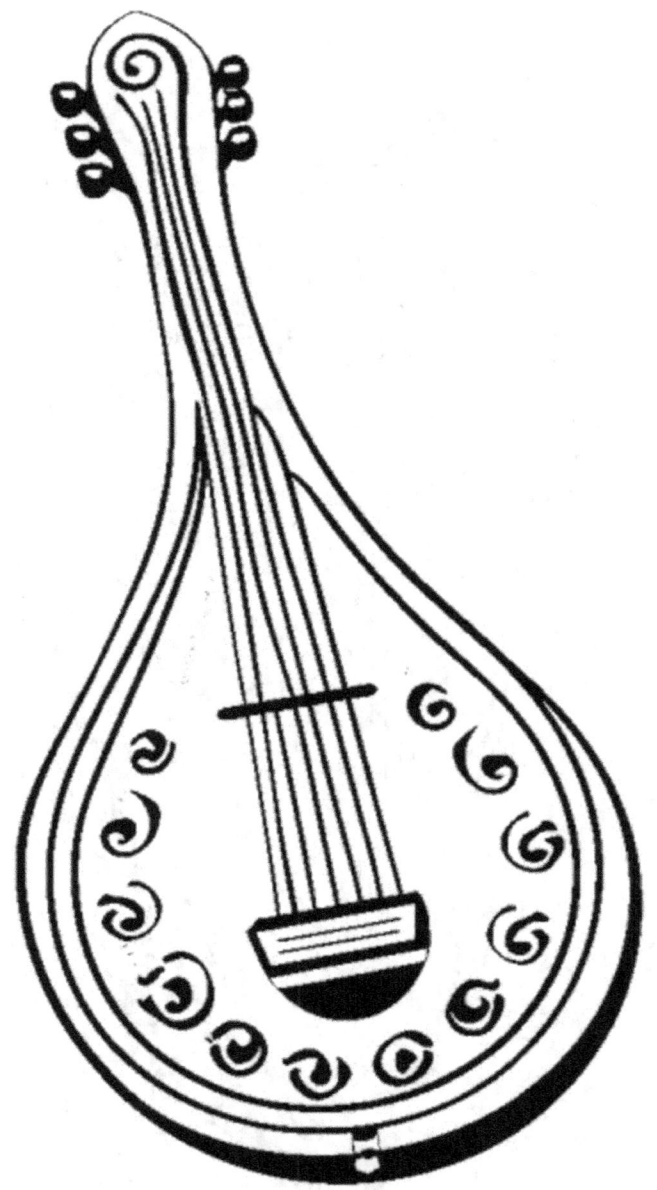

MANDOLIN

When scanning the QR code, you will be able to see the colored image and, if applicable, listen to the associated sound.

MUSICAL INSTRUMENTS

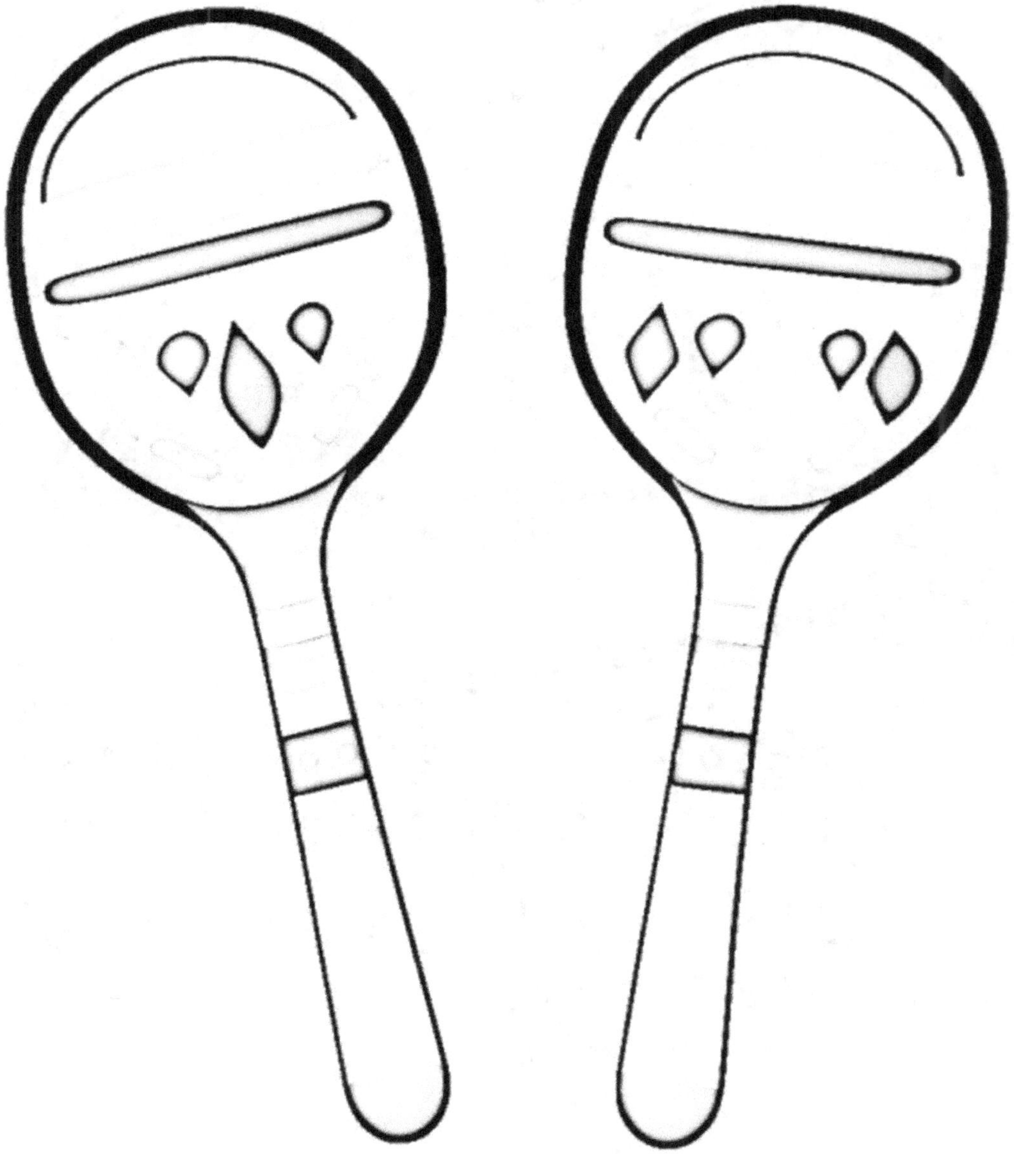

MARACAS

When scanning the QR code, you will be able to see the colored image and, if applicable, listen to the associated sound.

MUSICAL INSTRUMENTS

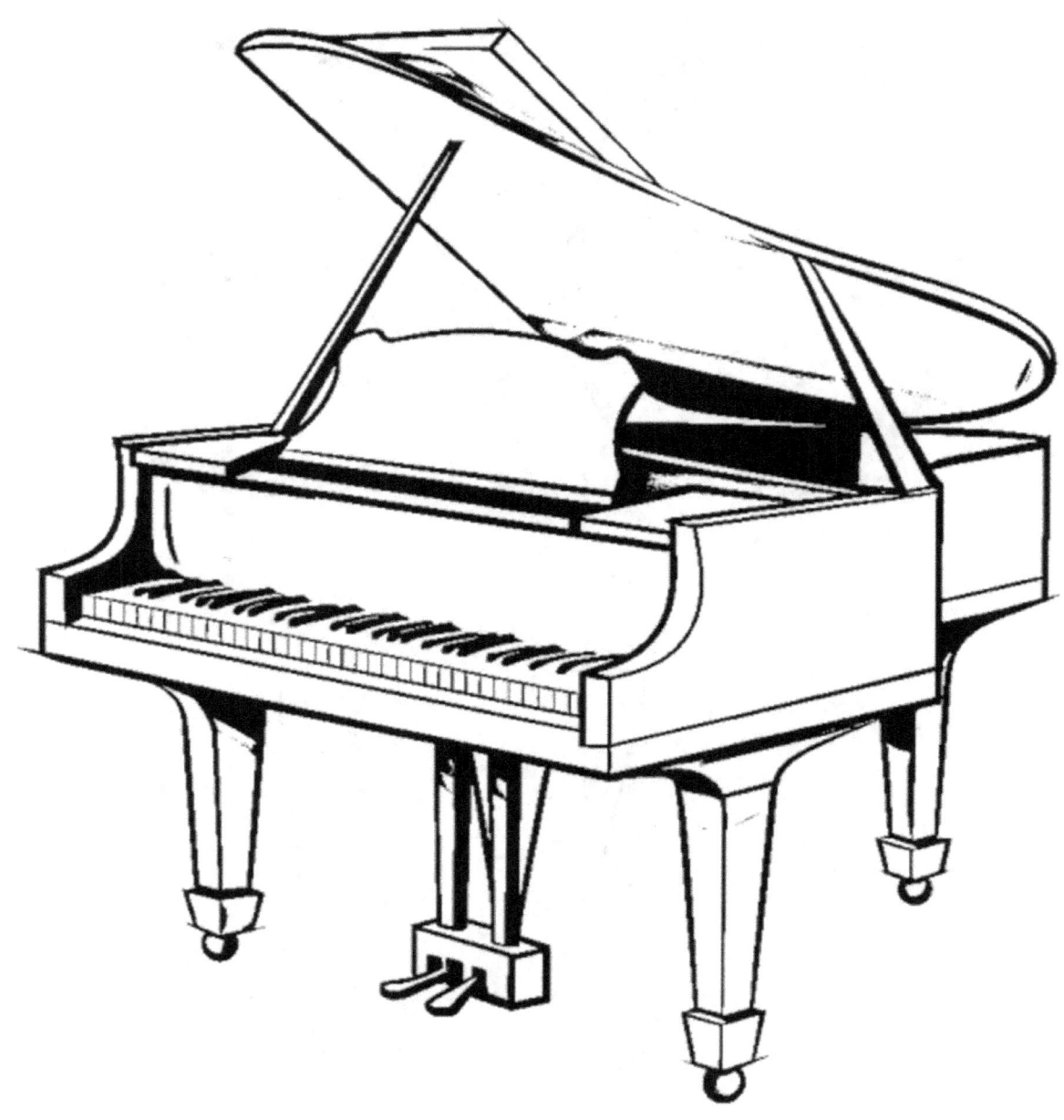

PIANO

When scanning the QR code, you will be able to see the colored image and, if applicable, listen to the associated sound.

MUSICAL INSTRUMENTS

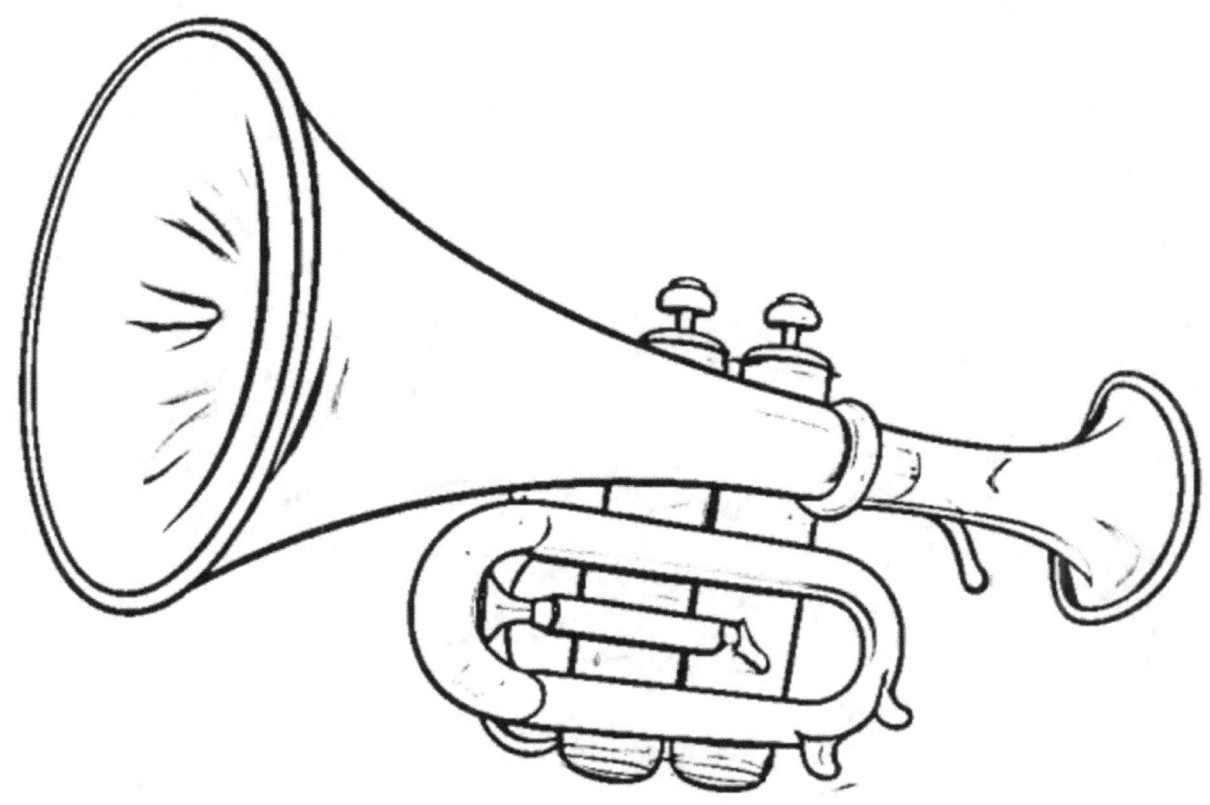

TRUMPET

When scanning the QR code, you will be able to see the colored image and, if applicable, listen to the associated sound.

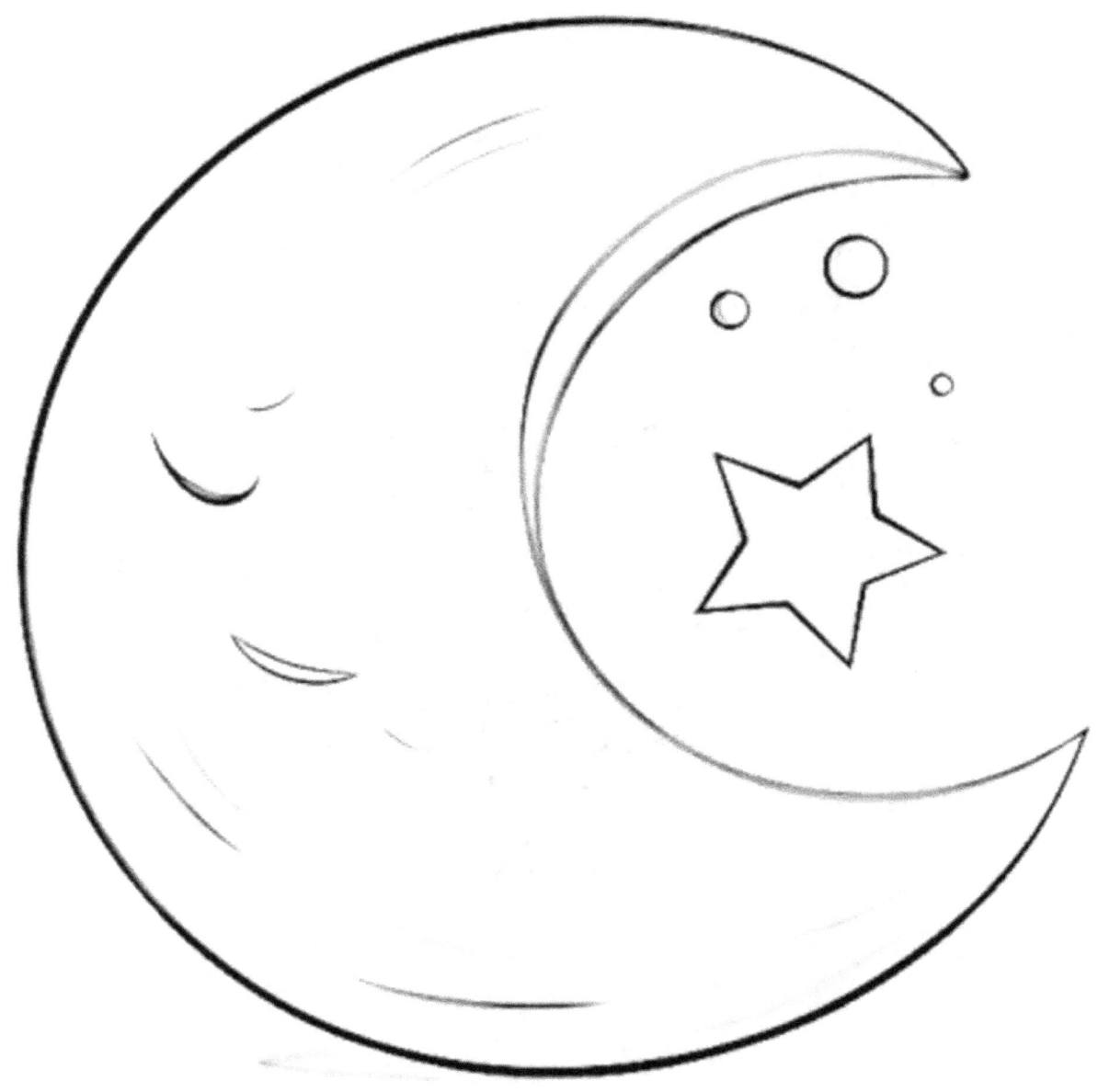

MOON

When scanning the QR code, you will be able to see the colored image and, if applicable, listen to the associated sound.

NATURE

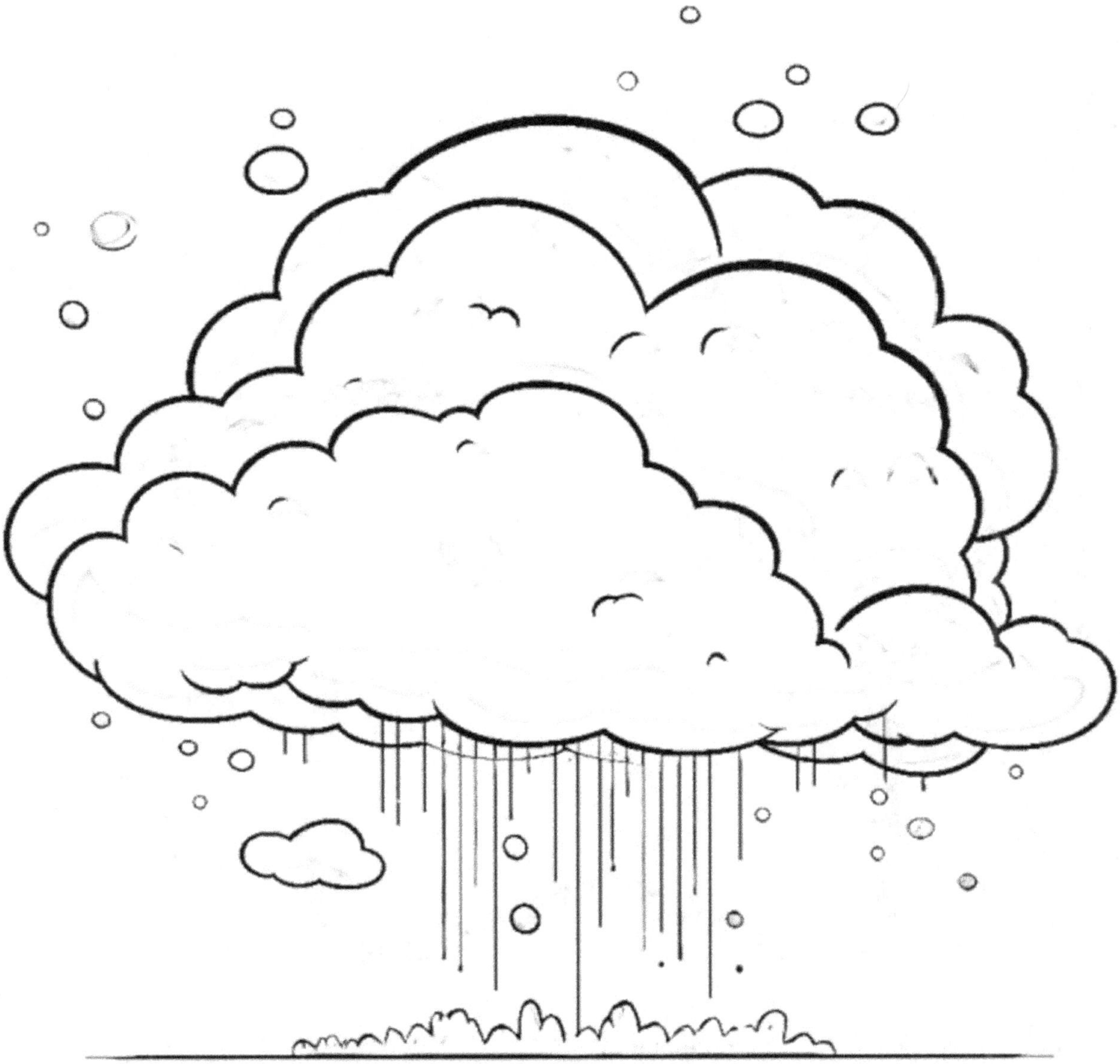

RAIN

When scanning the QR code, you will be able to see the colored image and, if applicable, listen to the associated sound.

NATURE

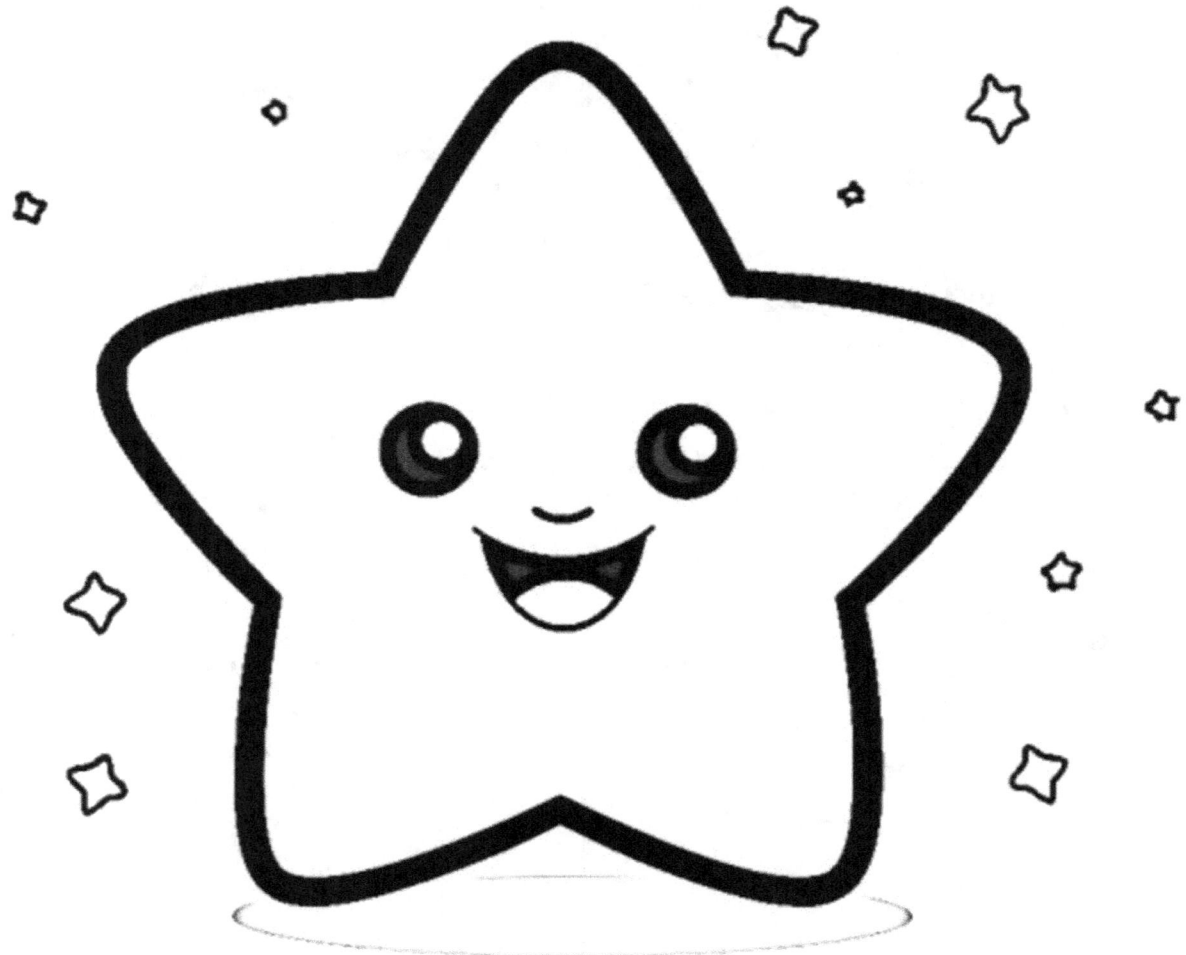

STAR

When scanning the QR code, you will be able to see the colored image and, if applicable, listen to the associated sound.

NATURE

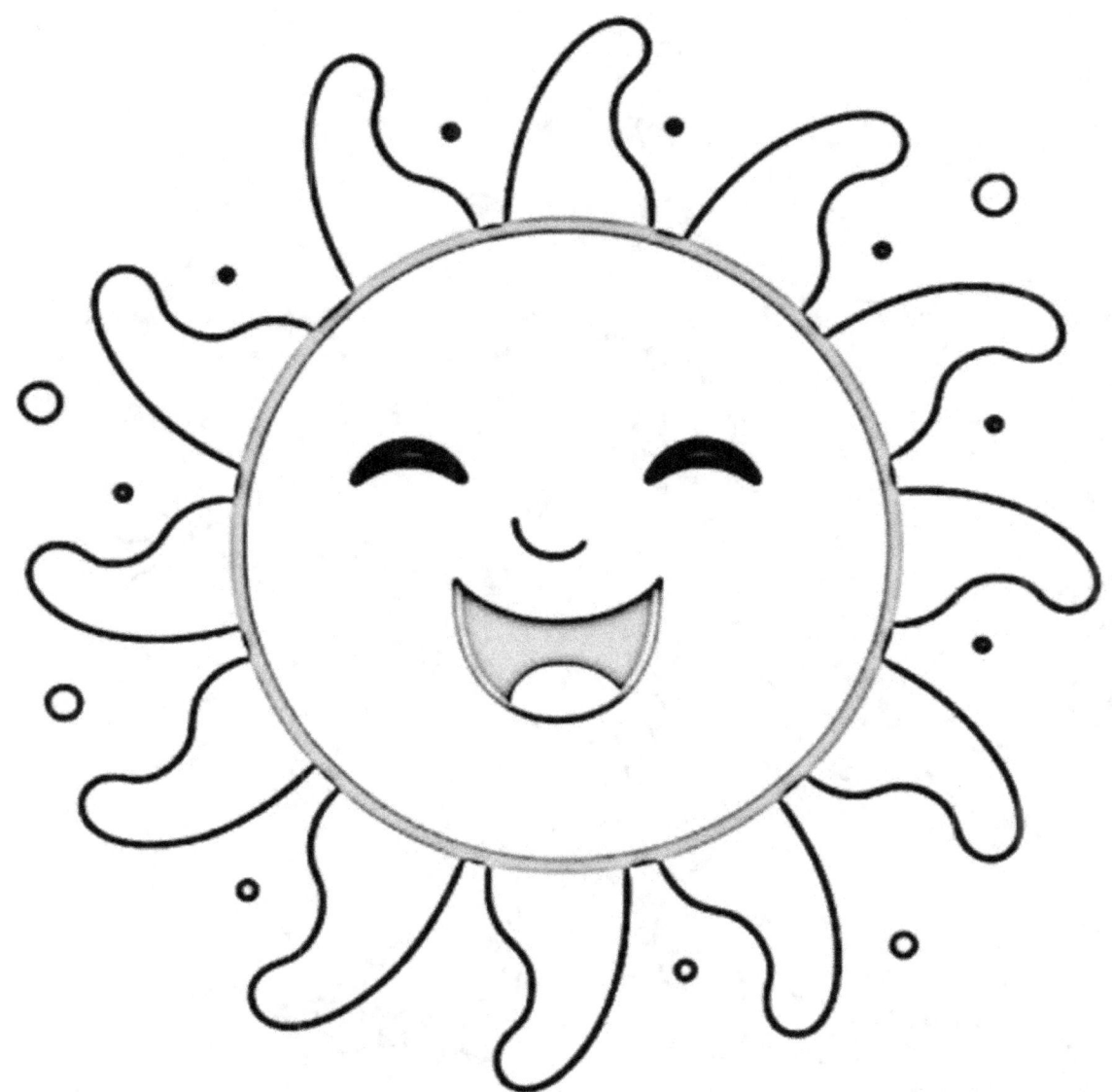

SUN

When scanning the QR code, you will be able to see the colored image and, if applicable, listen to the associated sound.

NATURE

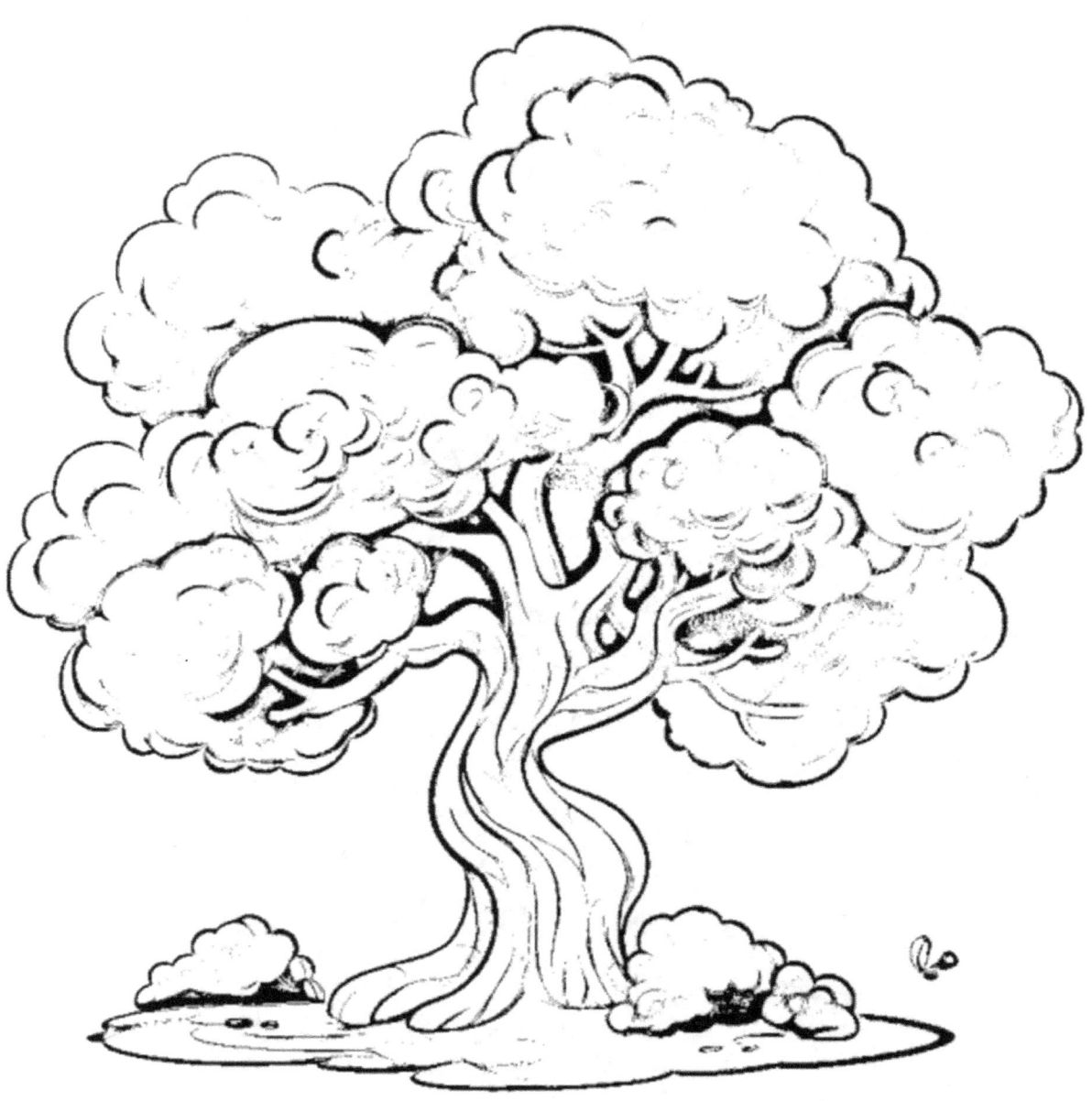

TREE

When scanning the QR code, you will be able to see the colored image and, if applicable, listen to the associated sound.

TRANSPORT

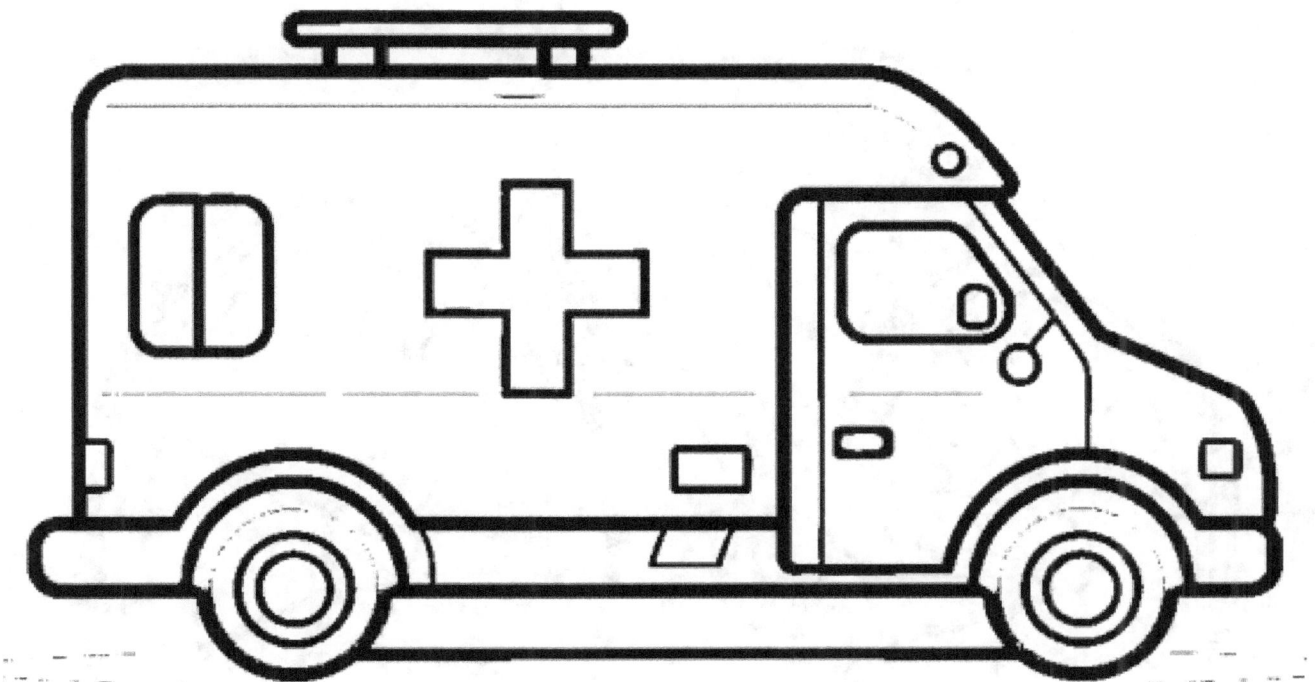

AMBULANCE

When scanning the QR code, you will be able to see the colored image and, if applicable, listen to the associated sound.

TRANSPORT

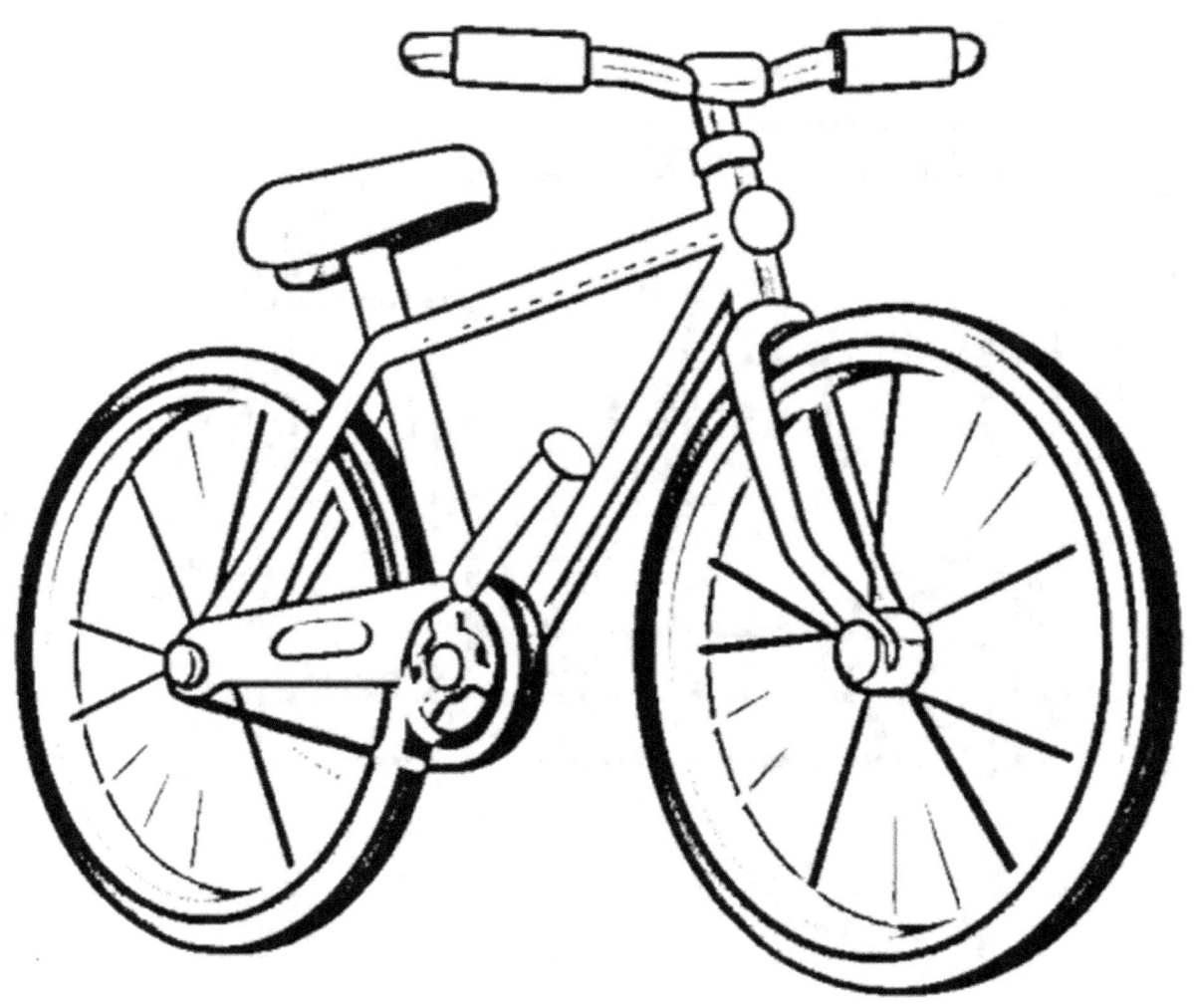

BICYCLE

When scanning the QR code, you will be able to see the colored image and, if applicable, listen to the associated sound.

TRANSPORT

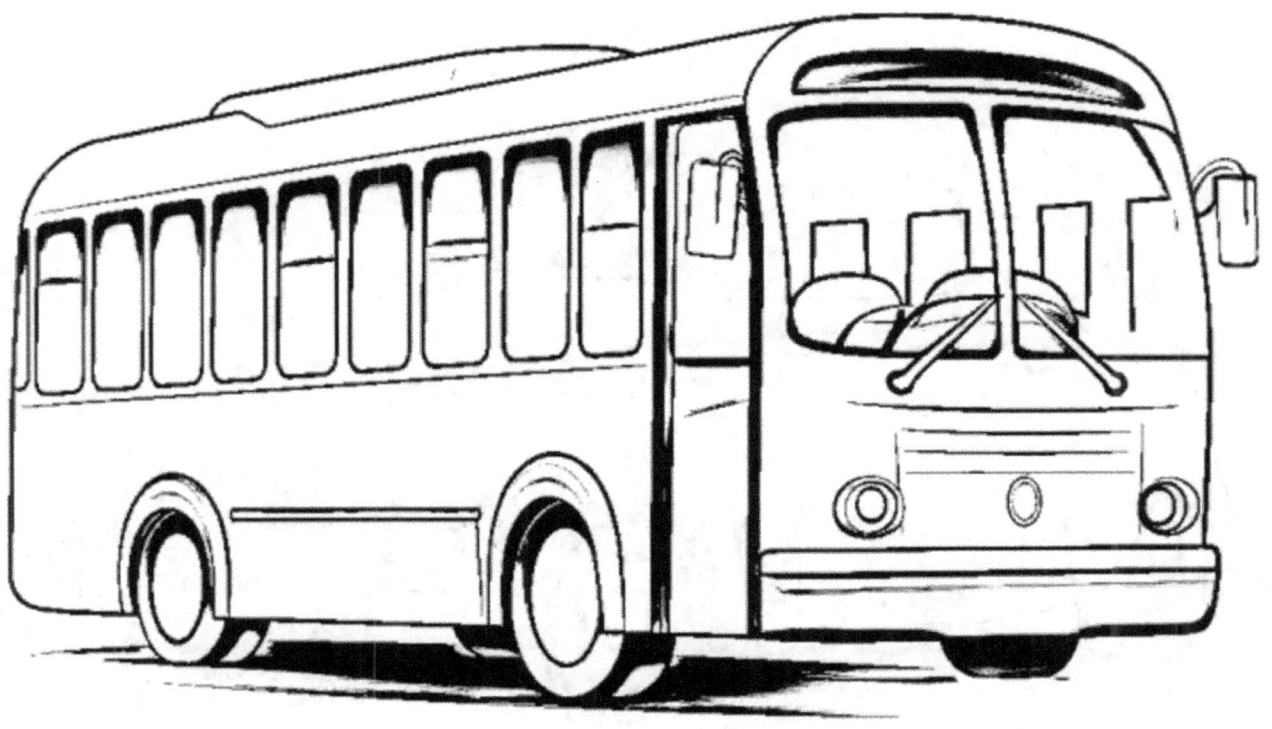

BUS

When scanning the QR code, you will be able to see the colored image and, if applicable, listen to the associated sound.

TRANSPORT

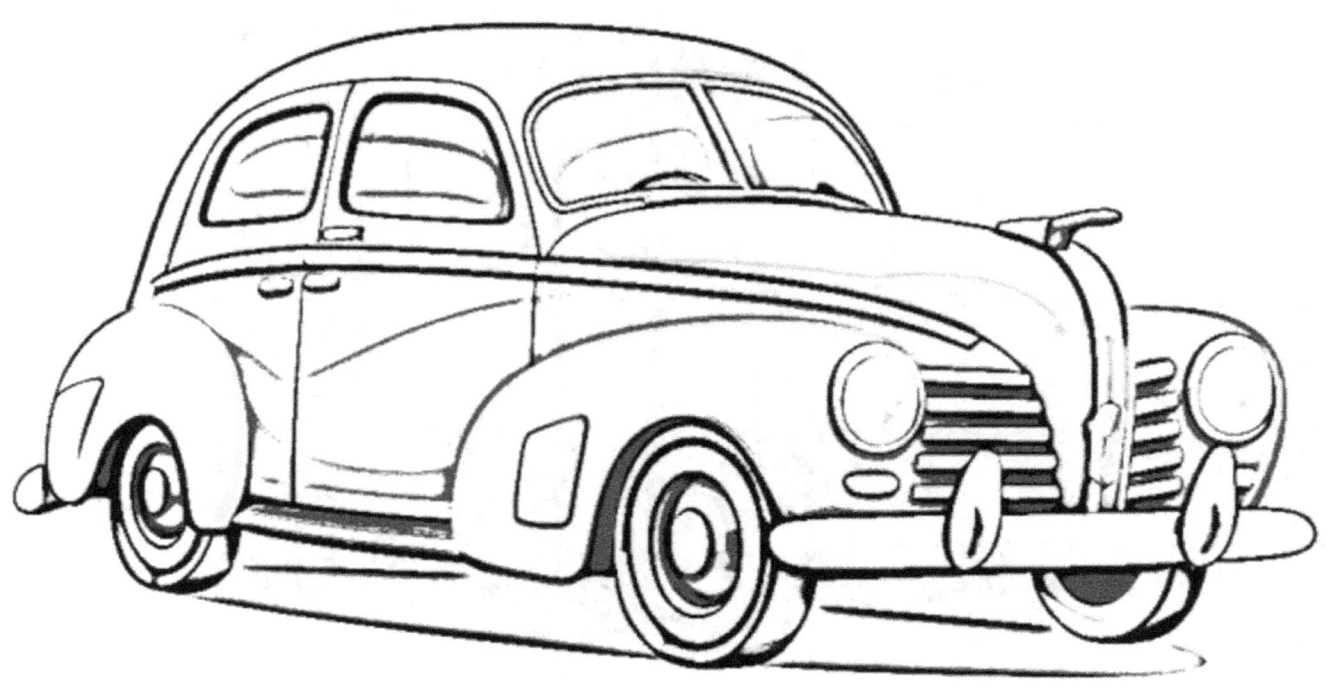

CAR

When scanning the QR code, you will be able to see the colored image and, if applicable, listen to the associated sound.

TRANSPORT

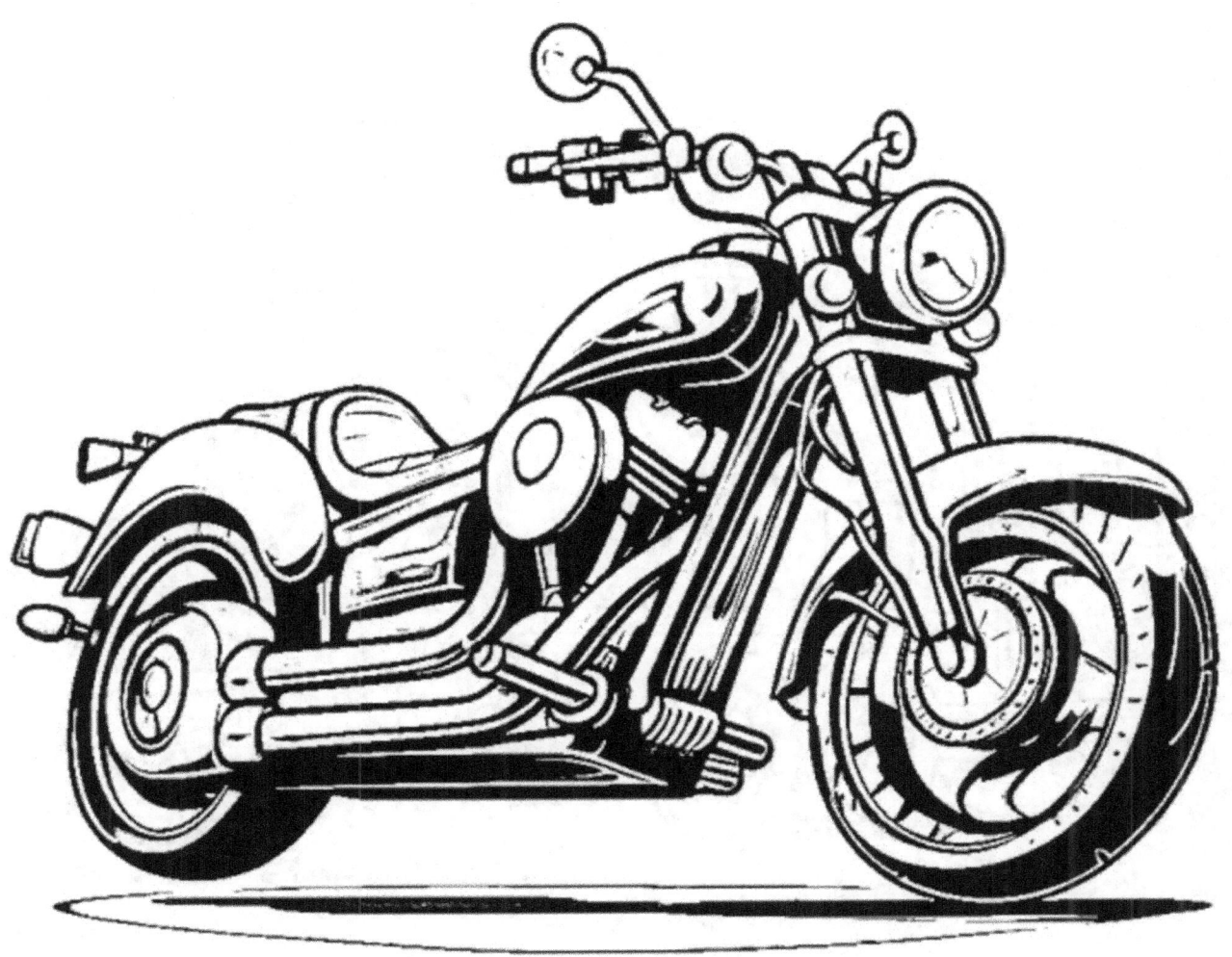

MOTORCYCLE

When scanning the QR code, you will be able to see the colored image and, if applicable, listen to the associated sound.

TRANSPORT

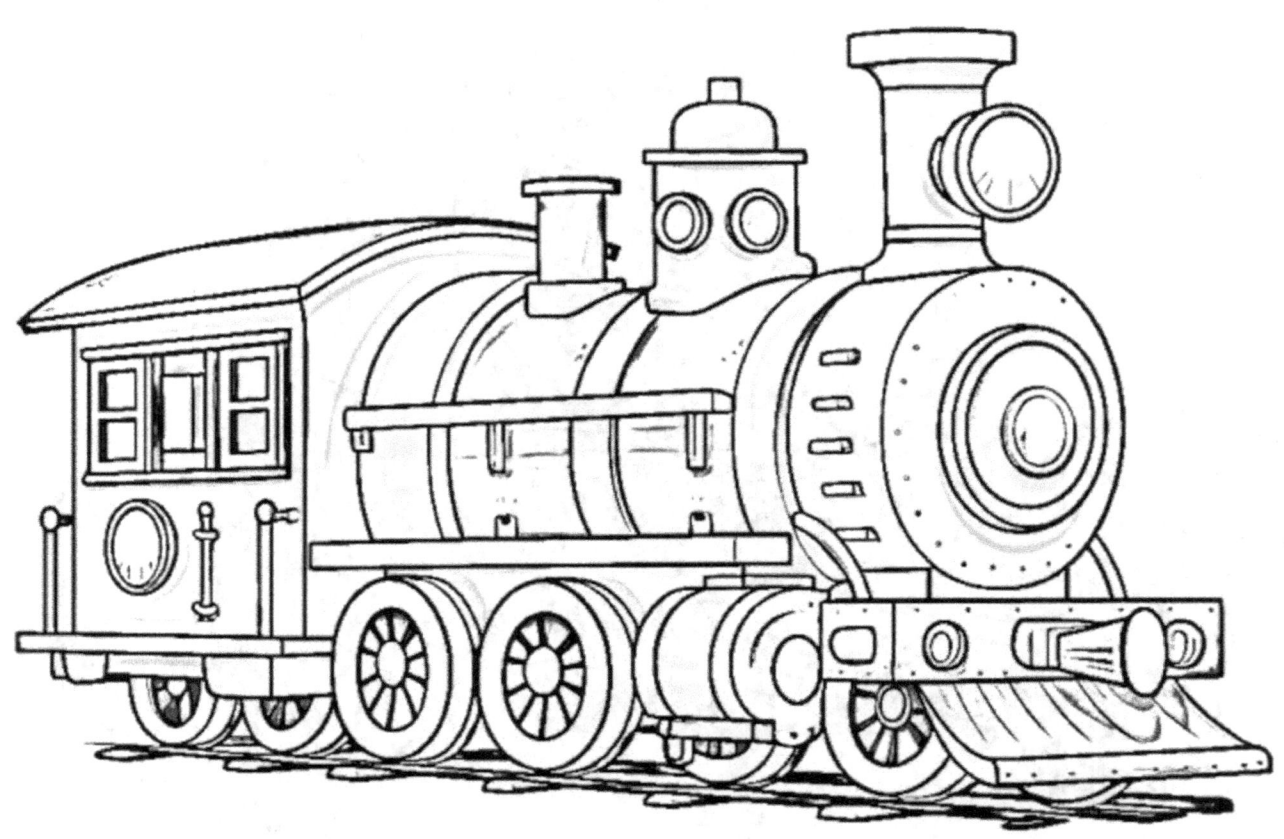

TRAIN

When scanning the QR code, you will be able to see the colored image and, if applicable, listen to the associated sound.

TRANSPORT

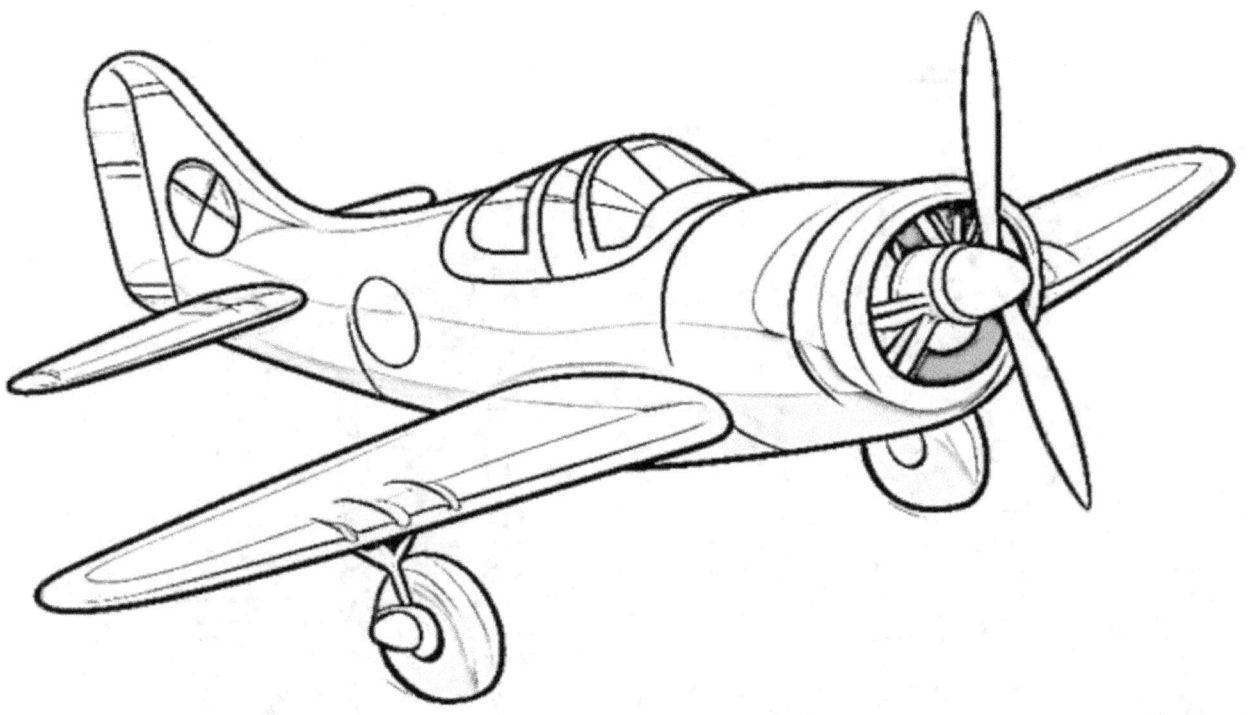

PLANE

When scanning the QR code, you will be able to see the colored image and, if applicable, listen to the associated sound.

TRANSPORT

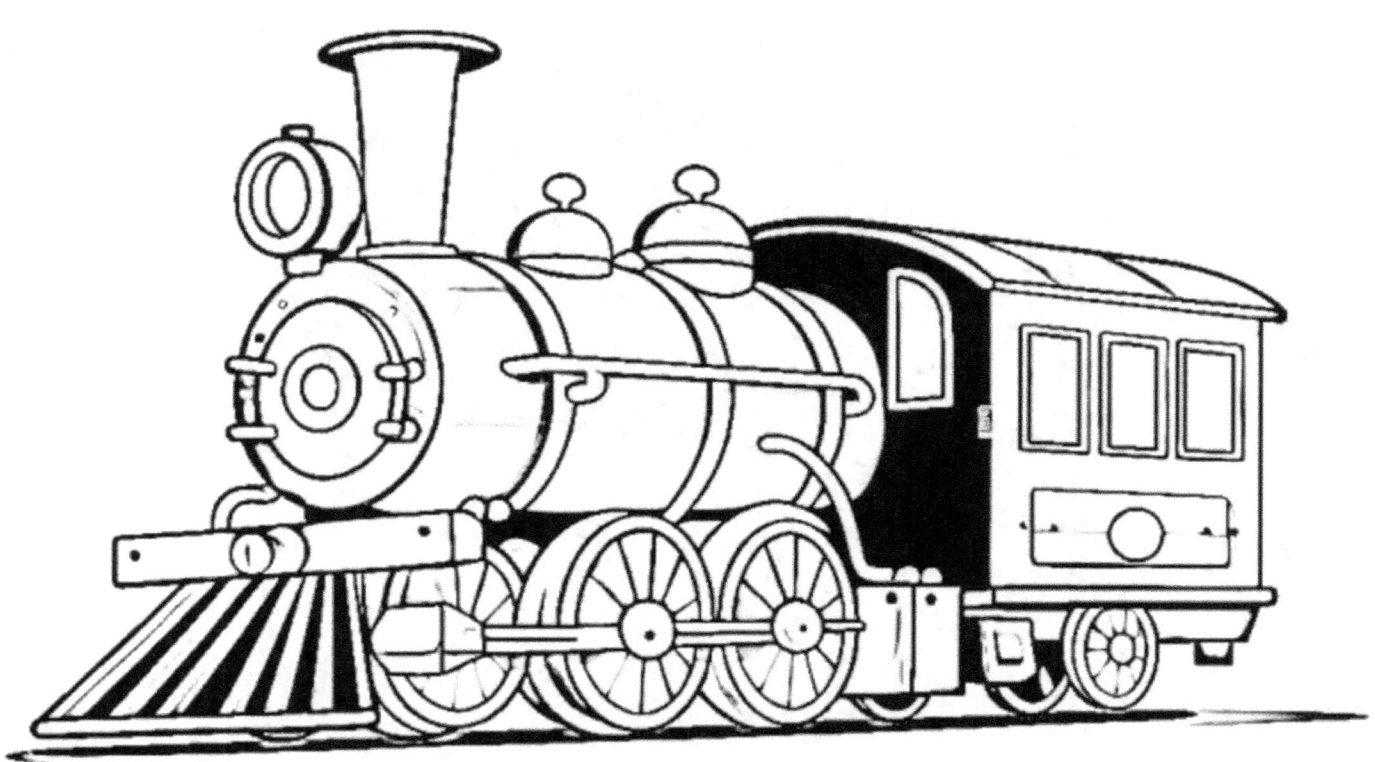

TRAIN

When scanning the QR code, you will be able to see the colored image and, if applicable, listen to the associated sound.

OTHERS

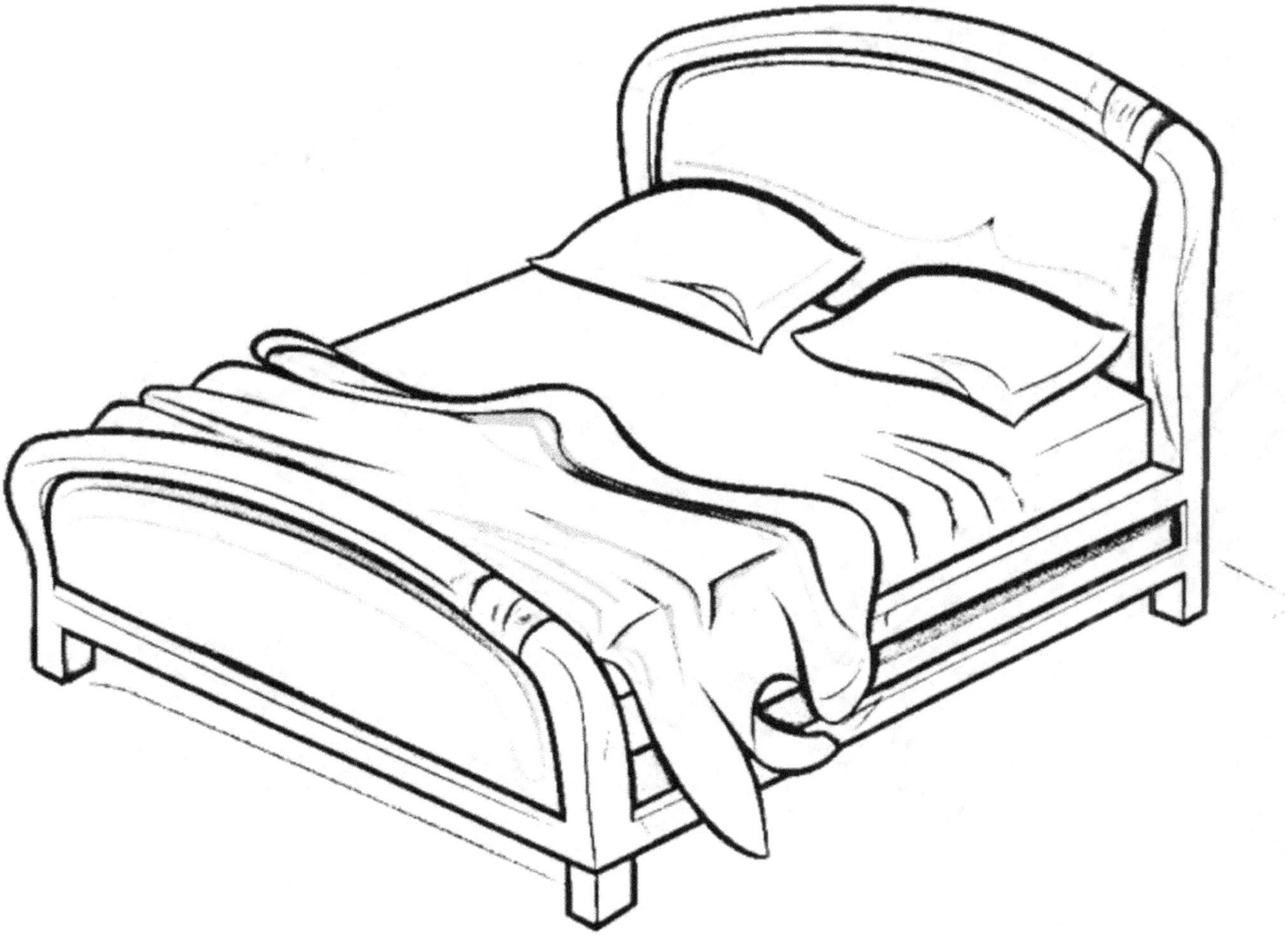

BED

When scanning the QR code, you will be able to see the colored image and, if applicable, listen to the associated sound.

OTHERS

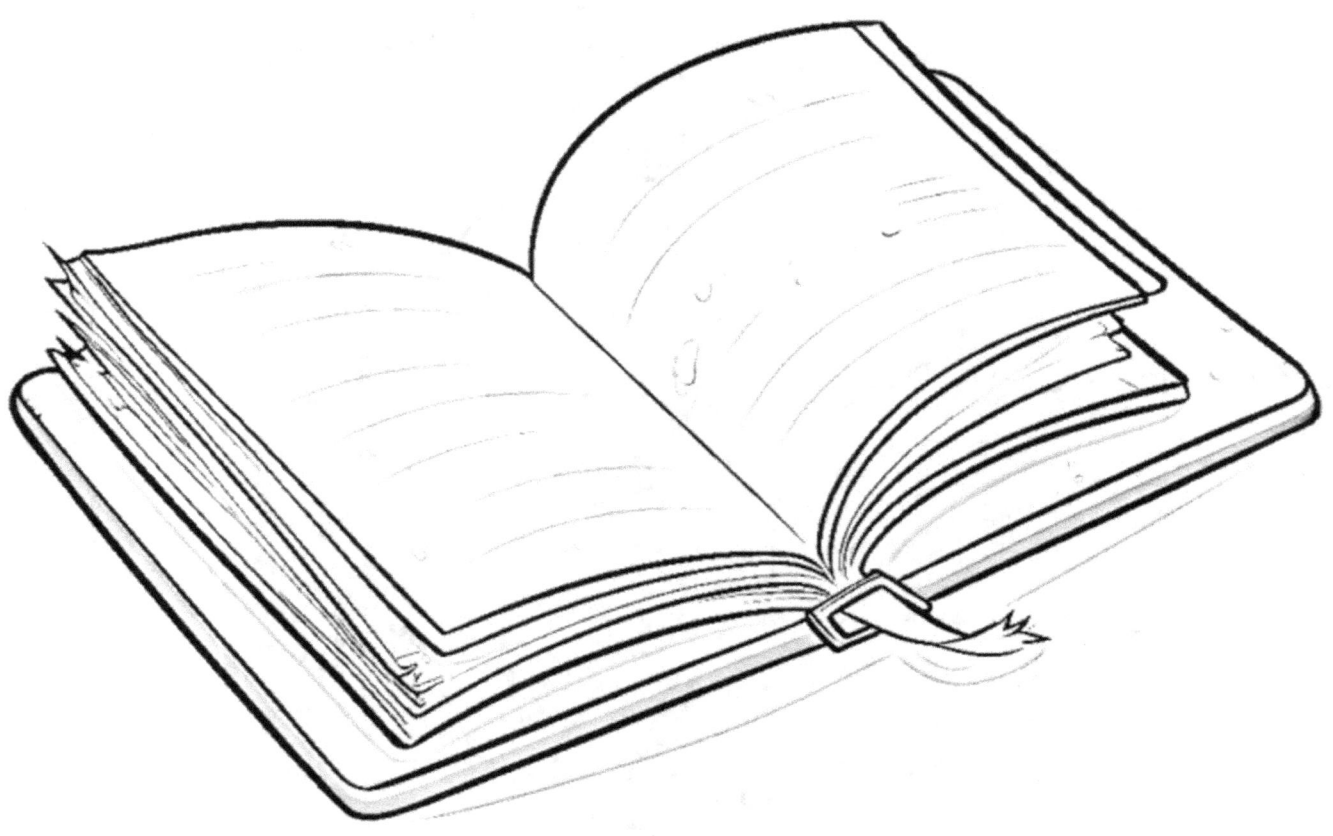

BOOK

When scanning the QR code, you will be able to see the colored image and, if applicable, listen to the associated sound.

OTHERS

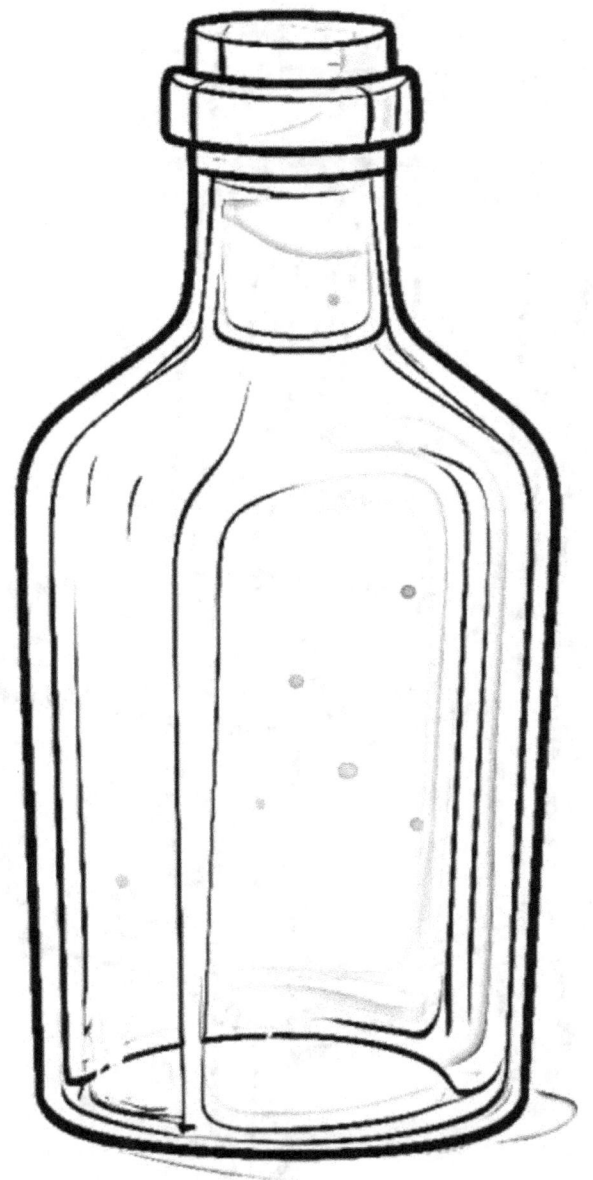

BOTTLE

When scanning the QR code, you will be able to see the colored image and, if applicable, listen to the associated sound.

OTHERS

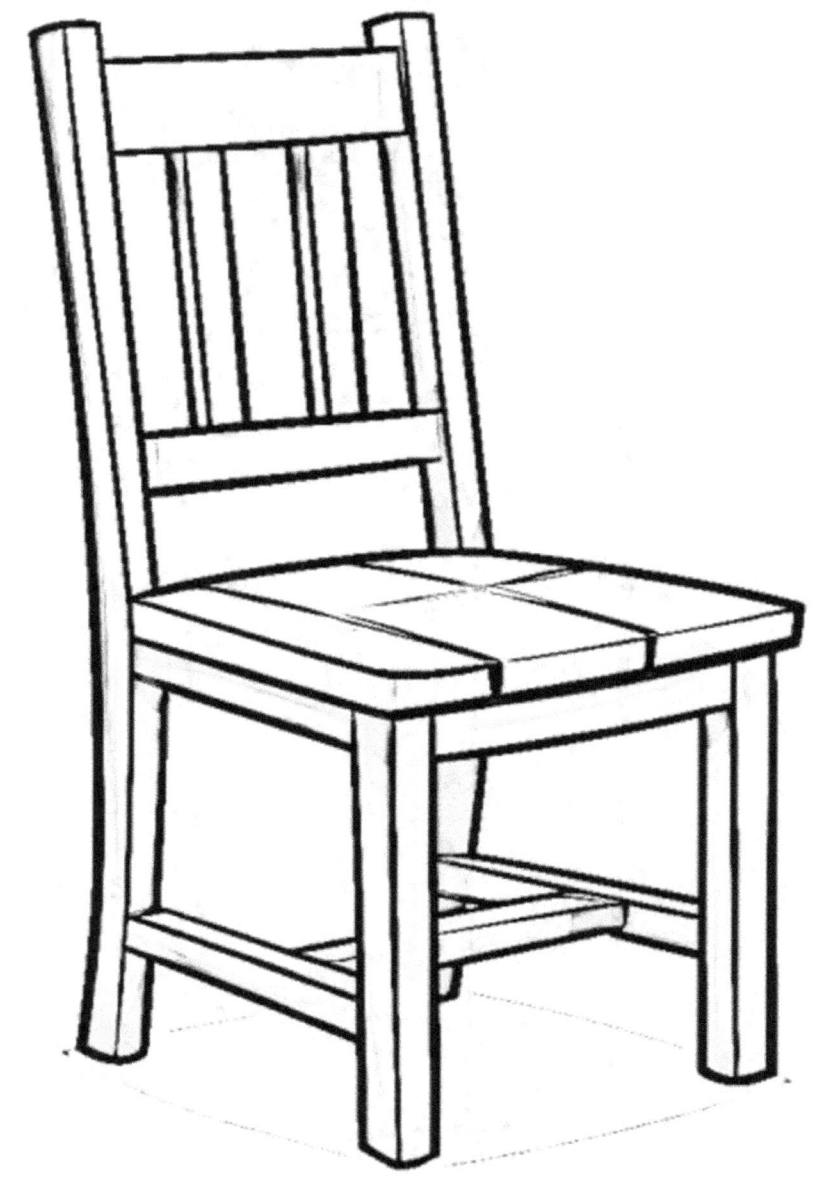

CHAIR

When scanning the QR code, you will be able to see the colored image and, if applicable, listen to the associated sound.

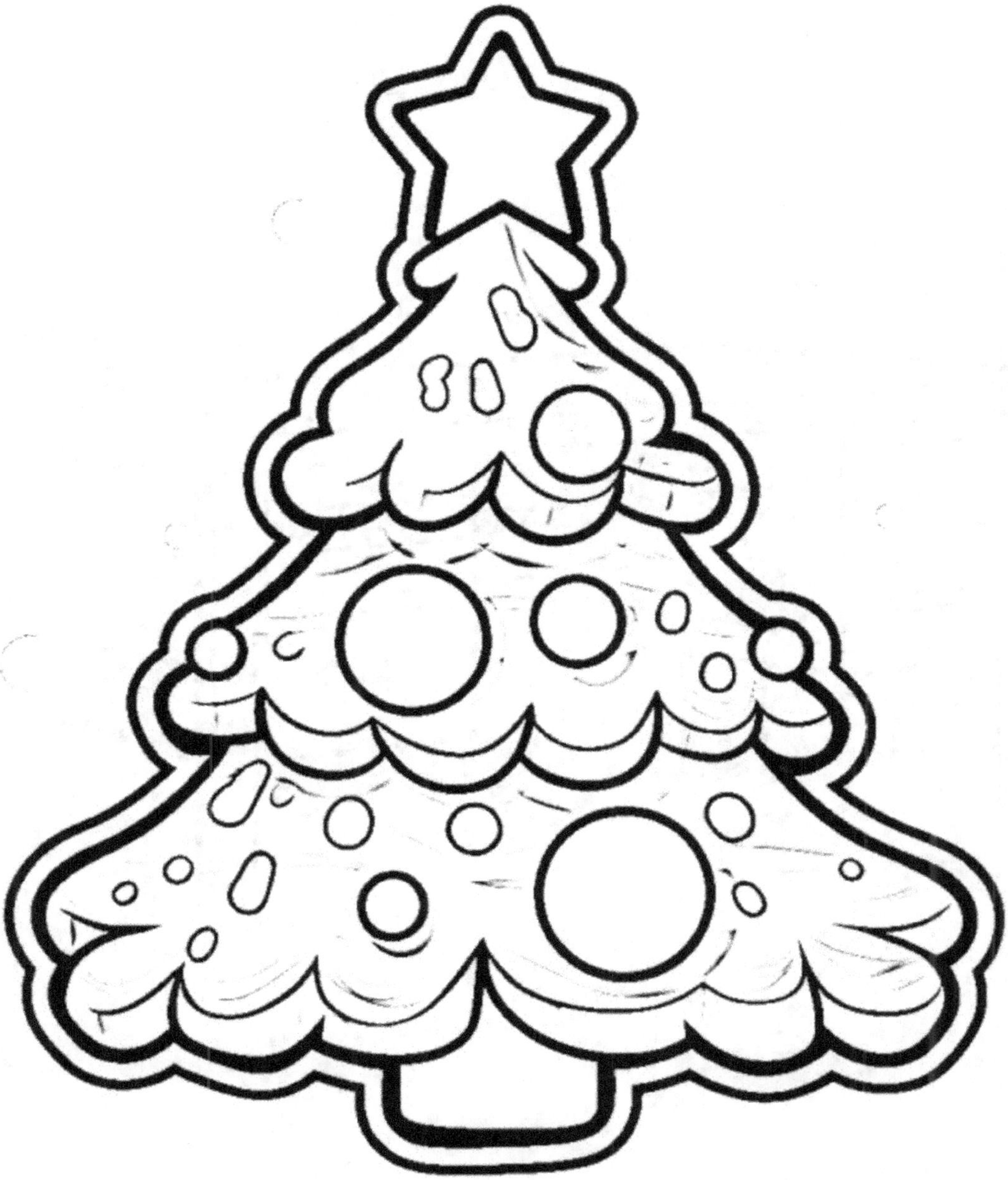

OTHERS

CRISTMAS TREE

When scanning the QR code, you will be able to see the colored image and, if applicable, listen to the associated sound.

OTHERS

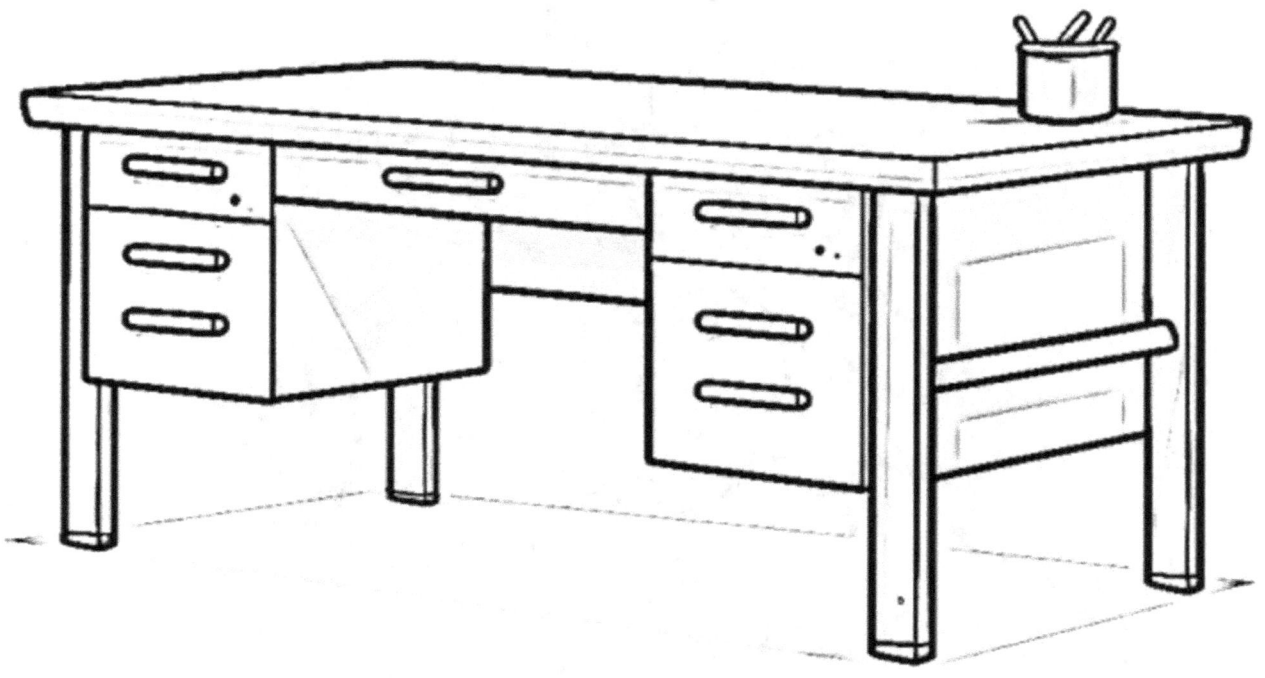

DESK

When scanning the QR code, you will be able to see the colored image and, if applicable, listen to the associated sound.

OTHERS

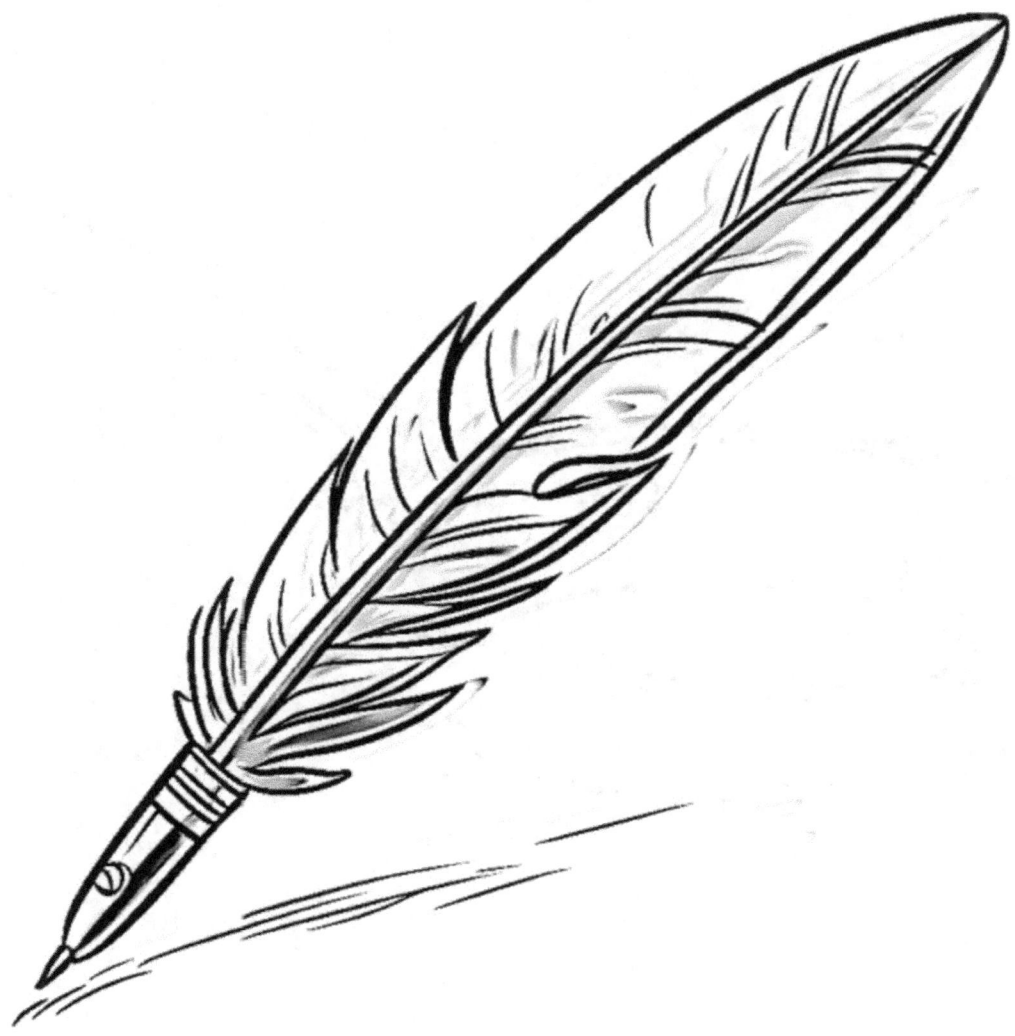

FEATHER

When scanning the QR code, you will be able to see the colored image and, if applicable, listen to the associated sound.

OTHERS

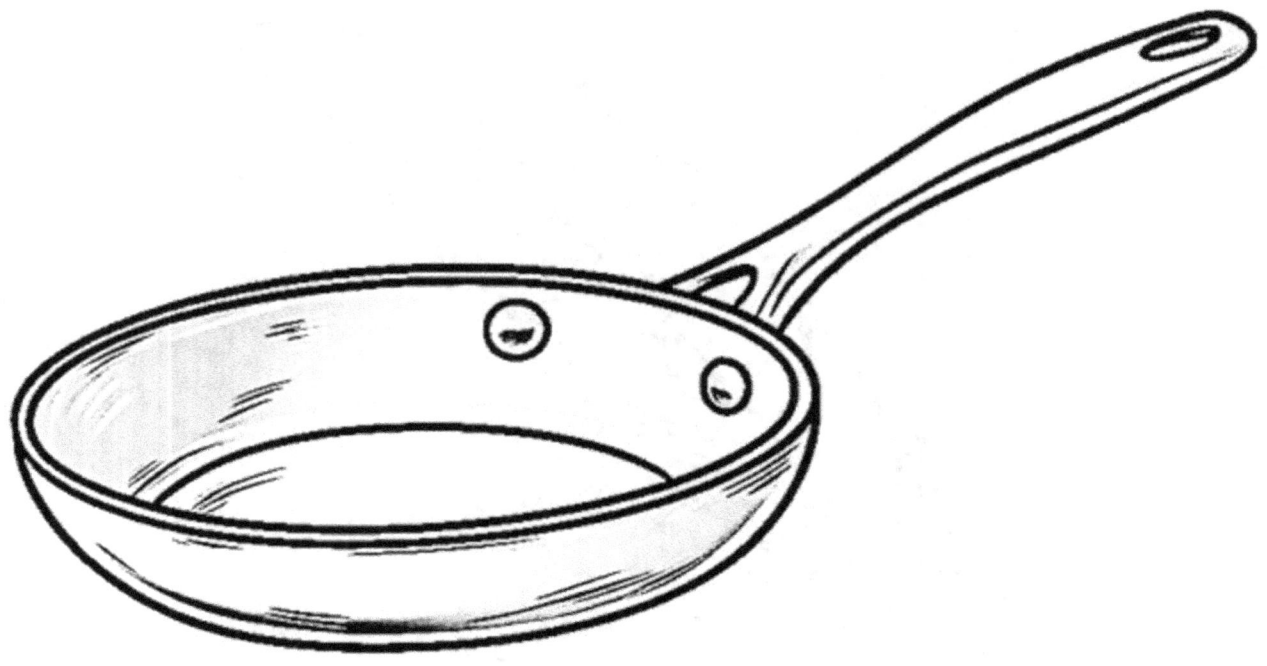

FRYING PAN

When scanning the QR code, you will be able to see the colored image and, if applicable, listen to the associated sound.

OTHERS

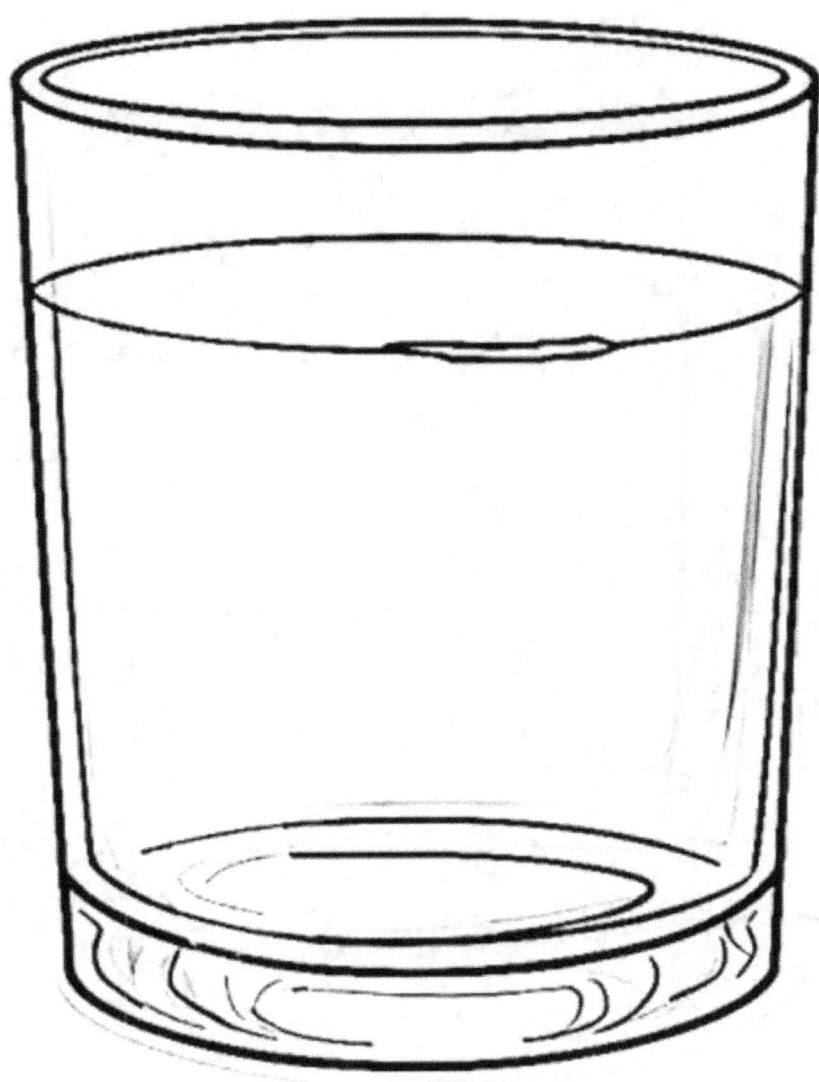

GLASS

When scanning the QR code, you will be able to see the colored image and, if applicable, listen to the associated sound.

OTHERS

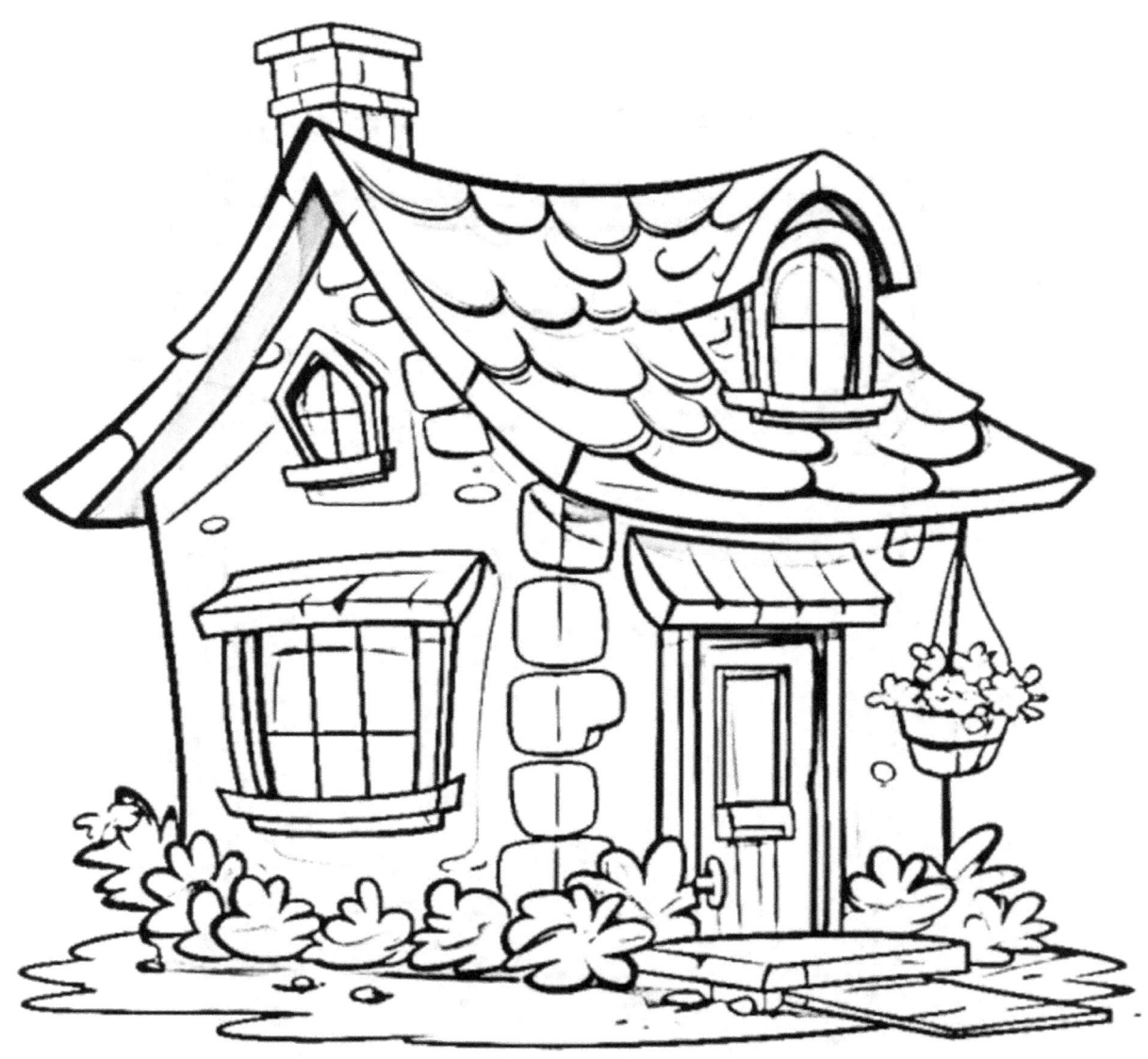

HOUSE

When scanning the QR code, you will be able to see the colored image and, if applicable, listen to the associated sound.

OTHERS

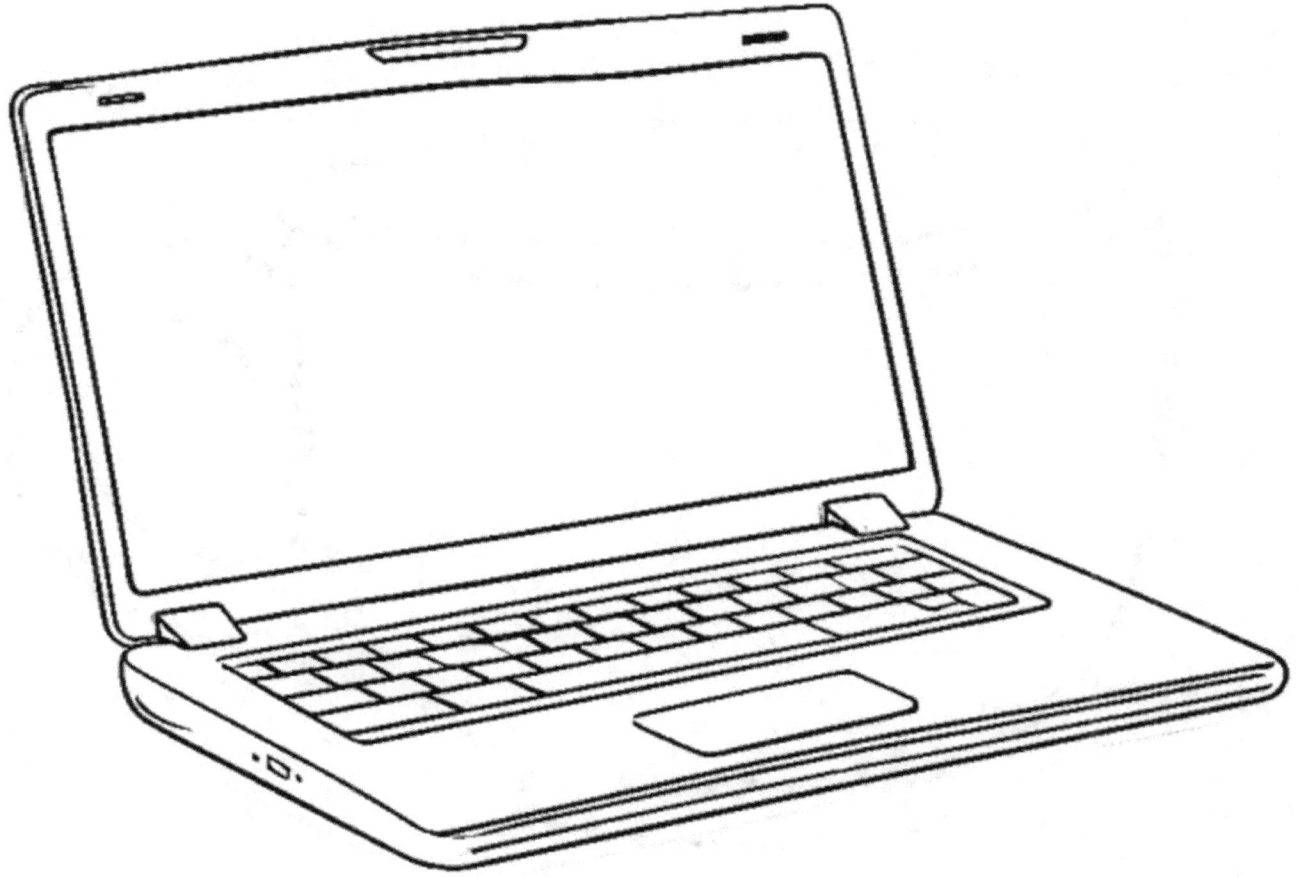

LAPTOP

When scanning the QR code, you will be able to see the colored image and, if applicable, listen to the associated sound.

OTHERS

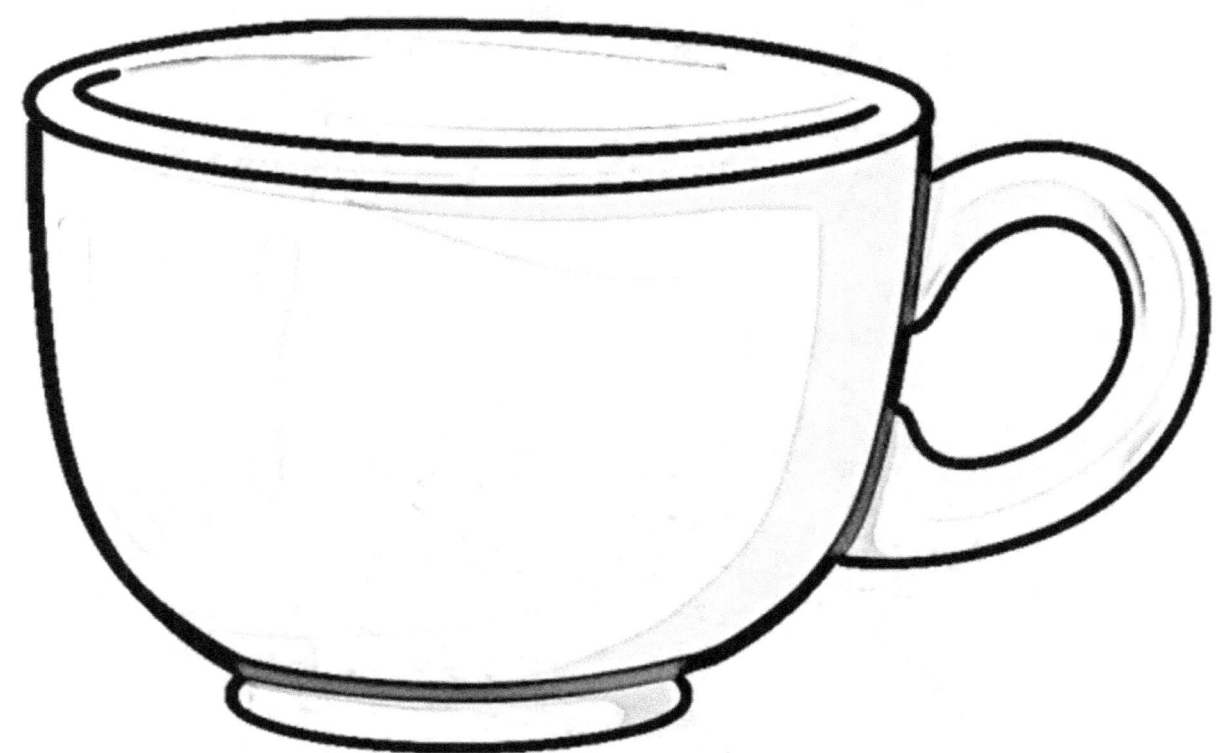

MUG

When scanning the QR code, you will be able to see the colored image and, if applicable, listen to the associated sound.

OTHERS

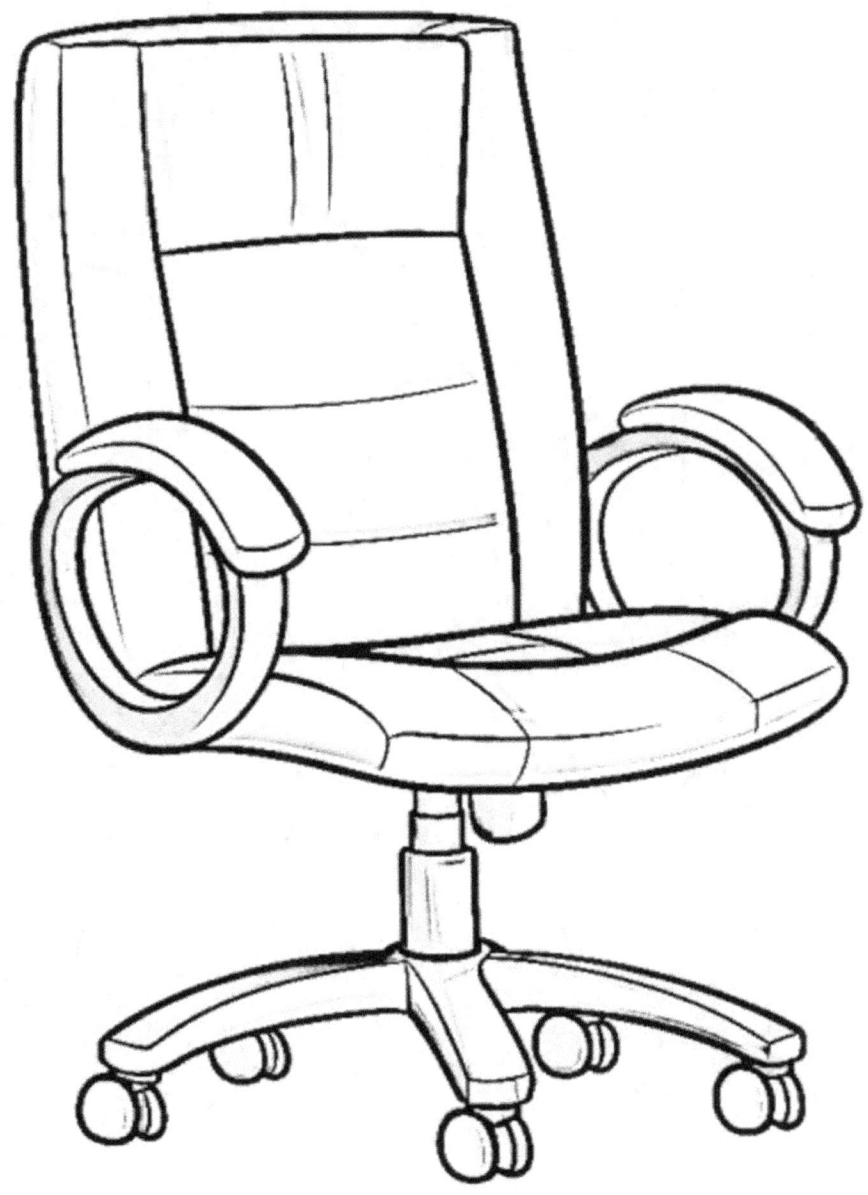

OFFICE CHAIR

When scanning the QR code, you will be able to see the colored image and, if applicable, listen to the associated sound.

OTHERS

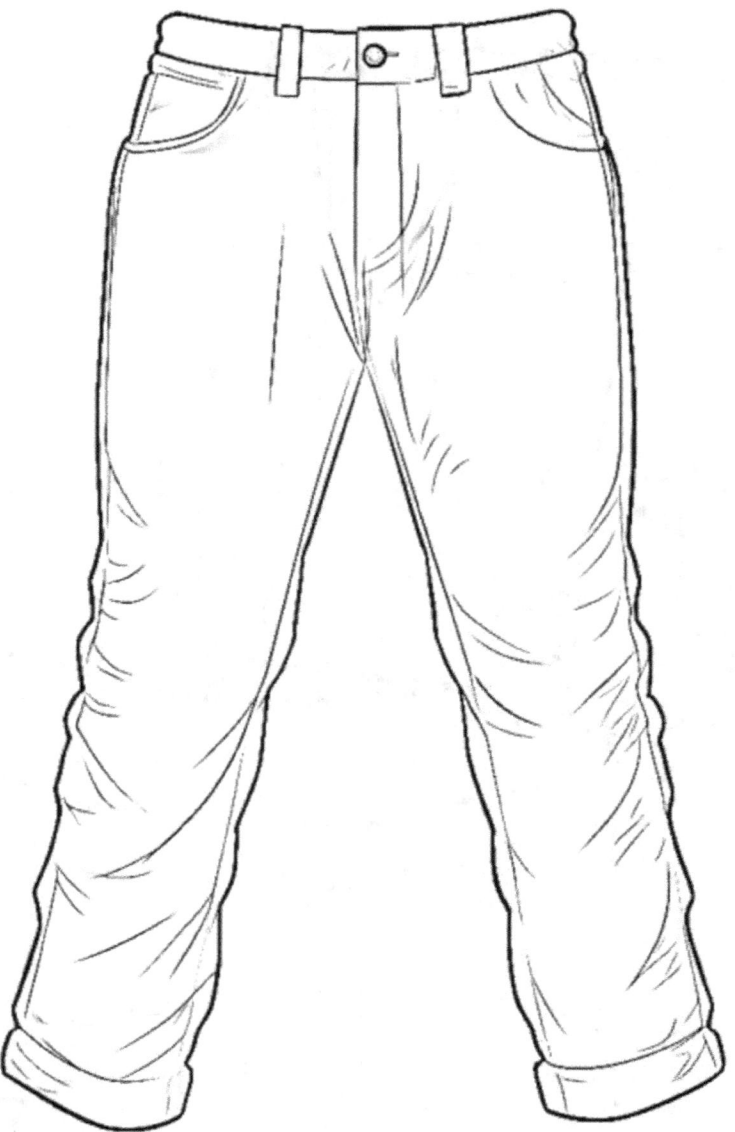

PANTS

When scanning the QR code, you will be able to see the colored image and, if applicable, listen to the associated sound.

OTHERS

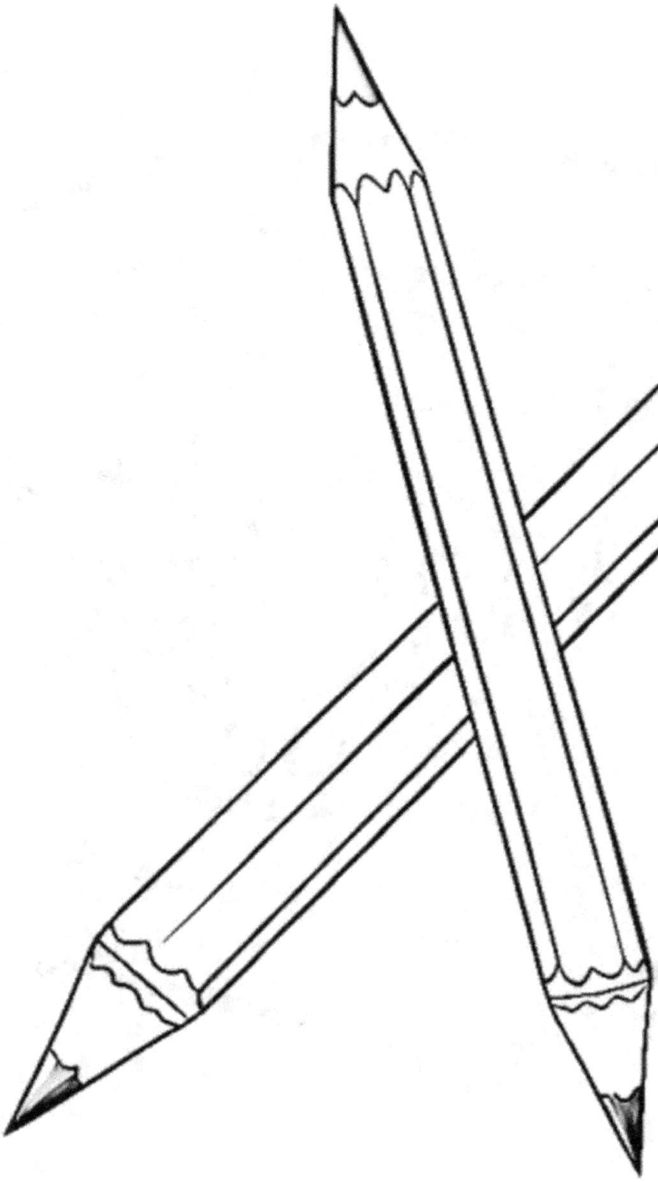

PENCILS

When scanning the QR code, you will be able to see the colored image and, if applicable, listen to the associated sound.

OTHERS

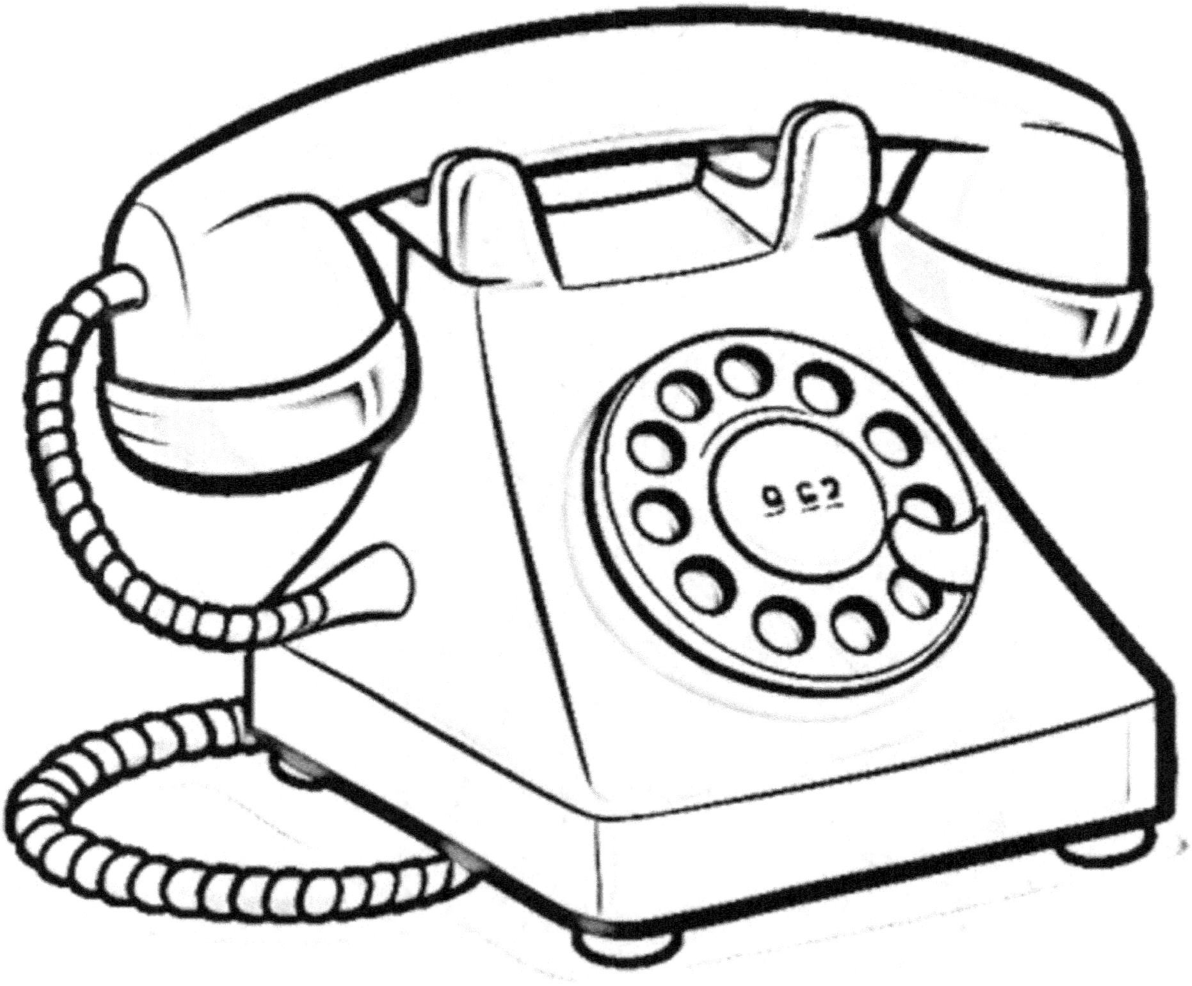

PHONE

When scanning the QR code, you will be able to see the colored image and, if applicable, listen to the associated sound.

OTHERS

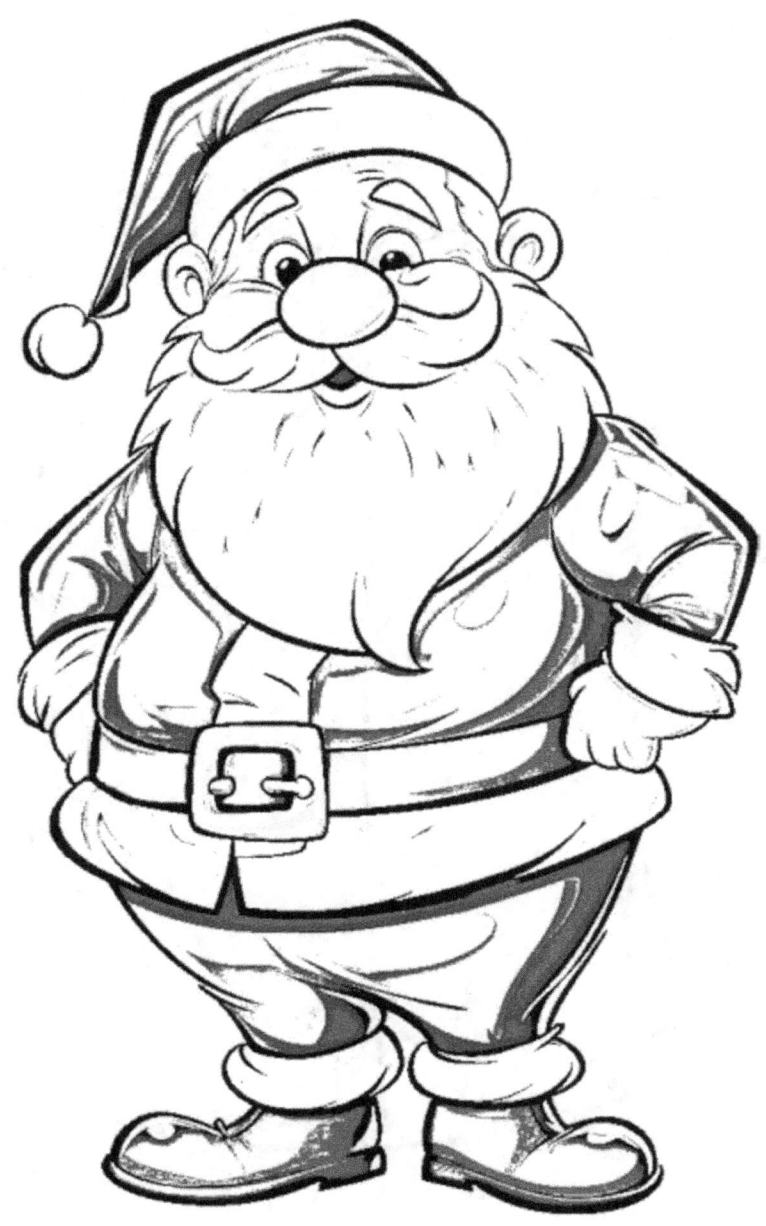

SANTACLOUS

When scanning the QR code, you will be able to see the colored image and, if applicable, listen to the associated sound.

OTHERS

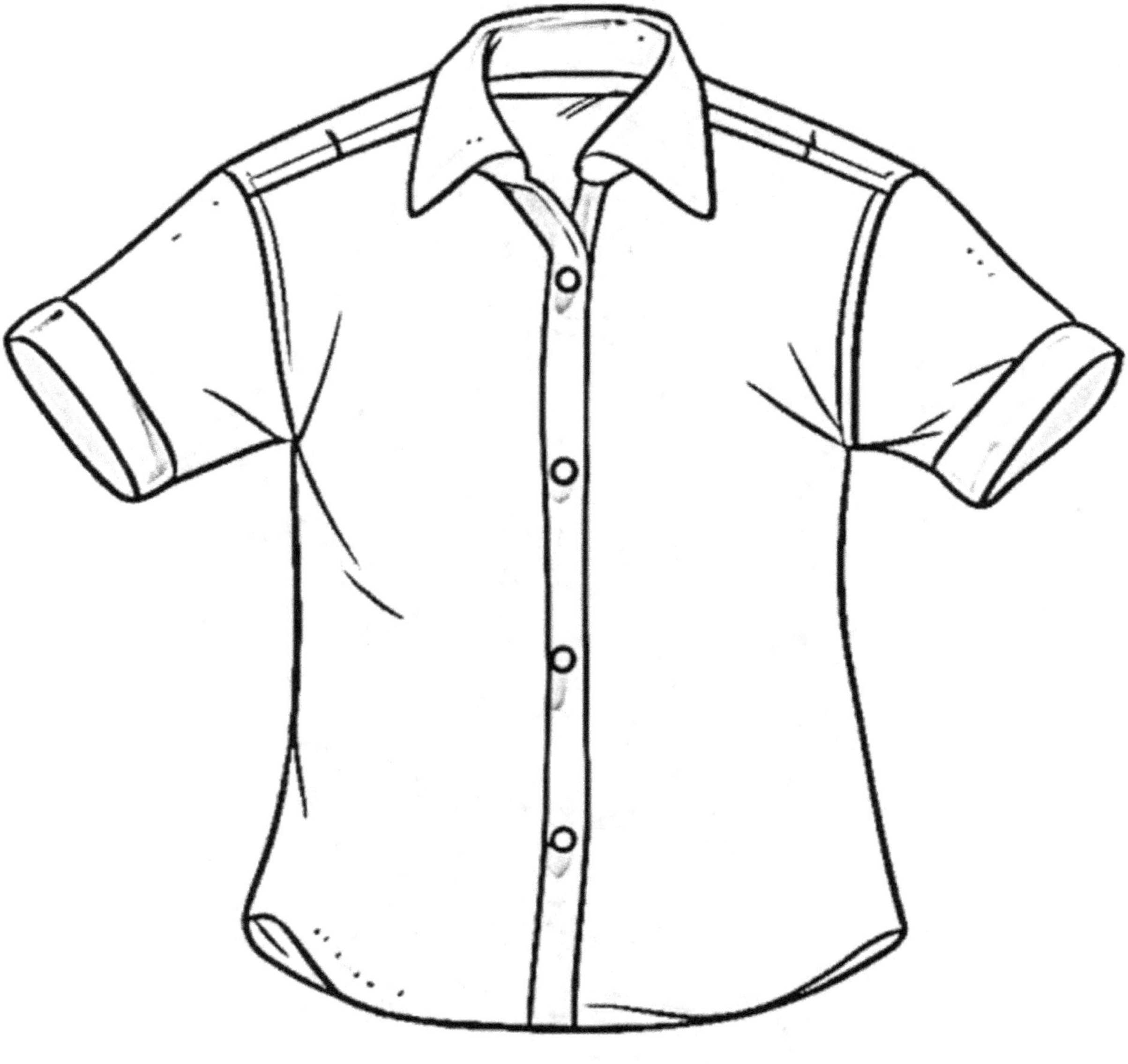

SHIRT

When scanning the QR code, you will be able to see the colored image and, if applicable, listen to the associated sound.

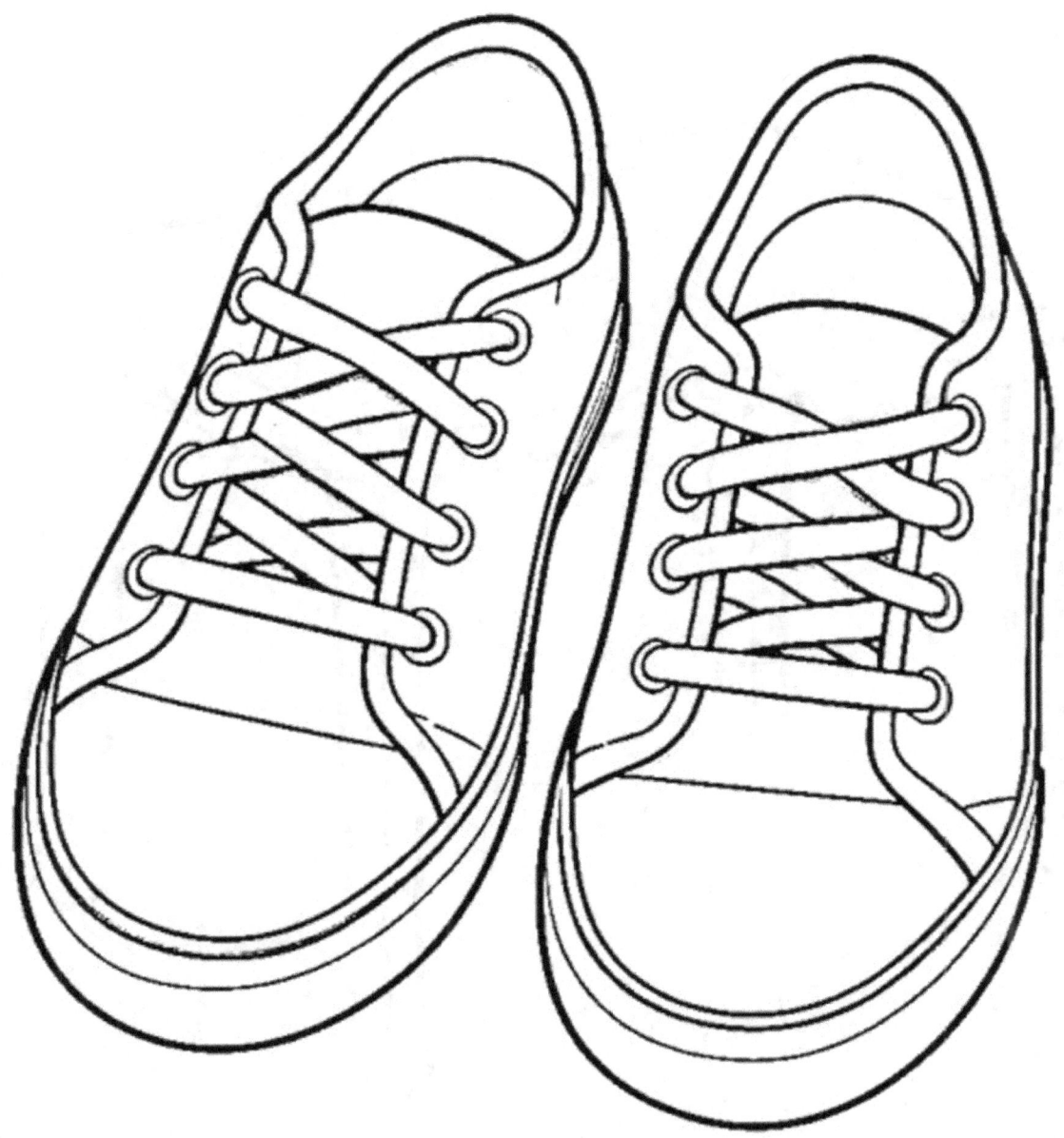

SHOES

When scanning the QR code, you will be able to see the colored image and, if applicable, listen to the associated sound.

OTHERS

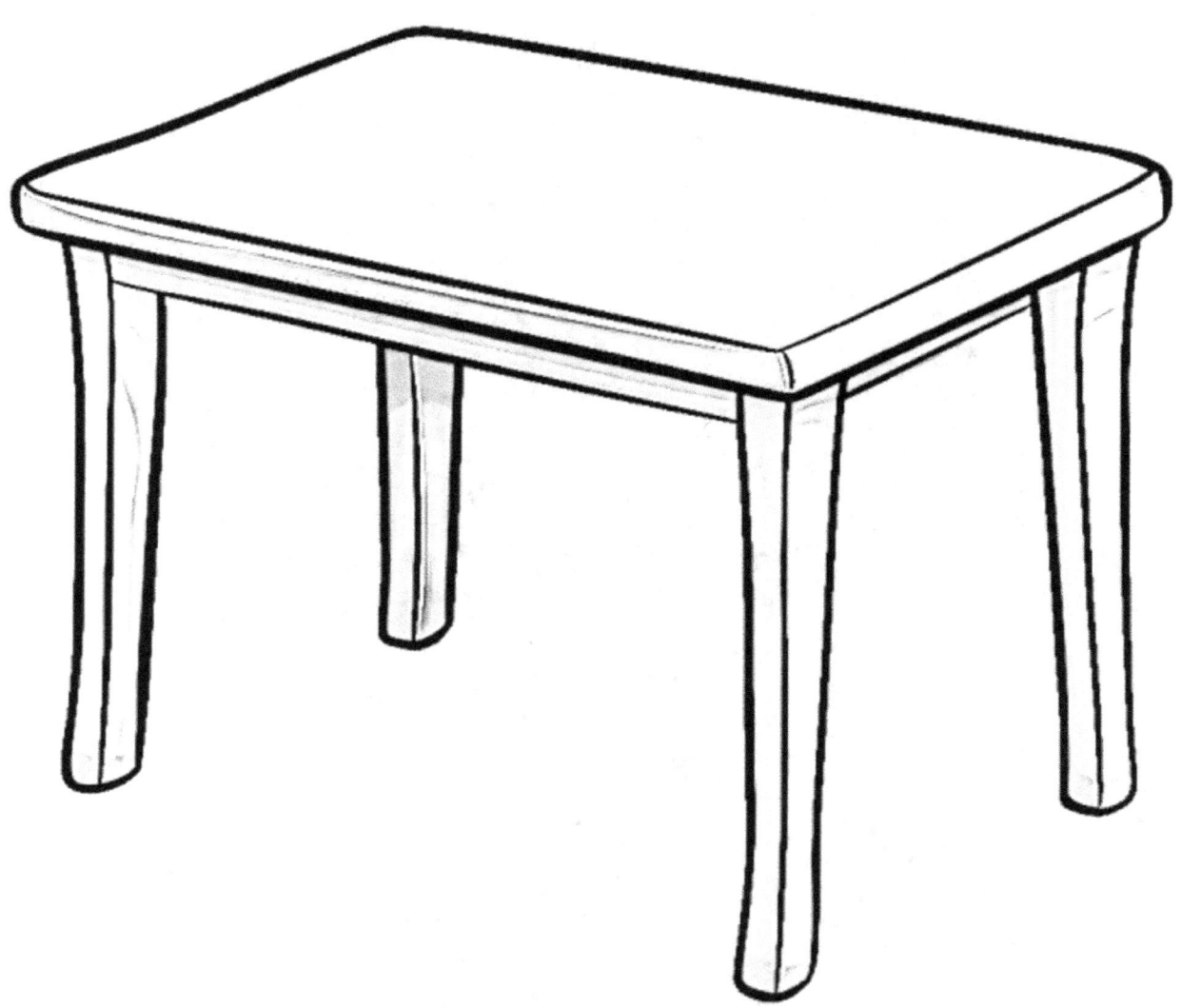

TABLE

When scanning the QR code, you will be able to see the colored image and, if applicable, listen to the associated sound.